MIMESIS
INTERNATIONAL

OUT OF SERIES

GW01085663

73-92
415-435
1. 8
ISBN: 9780198806530

ANDREW SPANNAUS

ORIGINAL SINS

Globalization, Populism,
and the Six Contradictions Facing
the European Union

MIMESIS
INTERNATIONAL

TABLE OF CONTENTS

AUTHOR'S PREFACE

Europe is in trouble. Or more precisely, the European Union is in trouble. Voters are increasingly supporting populist, non-mainstream parties, against the political establishment that has dominated the Western world over the past 40 years. It is all too common to hear that this process is due mostly to racist and reactionary views among significant portions of the population, and that the advance of "nationalism" is a harbinger for a return to war. Such arguments are not only simplistic, but often self-serving, useful for political and media elites to avoid discussing the fundamental problems facing Europe and the United States. The reality is that these problems are the result of a process of economic and financial globalization which on the whole has benefitted those who were already better off, while gradually hollowing out the middle class and hurting the poor.

The aim of this book is to, first, present the common economic thread behind the revolt of the voters, and then, in that context, assess the major arguments in favor of integration among European countries on the model of the European Union. Ultimately, the question is whether the EU in its current form can survive, or if a populist uprising will force countries to take a step back, and rethink the process of integration. I present six contradictions in particular that Europeans must address one way or another, whether they wish to strengthen their alliance, or only hope to continue peaceful cooperation through a looser structure. Today, more than ever, what is needed is a serious discussion of the concept of sovereignty, i.e. the role of nation-states – or even larger entities – with respect to other forces that affect the organization of society.

This is not an academic work, and thus the book does not go into great technical detail regarding economic subjects such as trade, inequality, and falling living standards. Some notes and links are provided in the footnotes, but for those who wish to see more, there is an abundance of evidence available to the public, from popular books to statistics on purchasing power and labor conditions over the past several decades.

There are, of course, some "serious people" who deny that things are worse now than they were 20, 30, or 40 years ago. I'll leave that argument for elsewhere, in part because what neoliberal economists conclude based on strained interpretations of the numbers, has little bearing on the voting decisions of millions of people struggling to make ends meet. To the contrary, telling people that they are imagining their difficulties usually just exacerbates the problem. The task here is to show how reactions to globalization are driving the threat to political and institutional stability, through a clear assessment of the process that is before our eyes, although many still refuse to see it.

Two more points before getting started. The first regards the role of immigration politics. Opposition to immigration gets a lot of attention, making it easy to point to racist attitudes to brand protest movements as bigoted and *deplorable*, so to speak. It's more challenging to look at the broader process that provides the critical mass for the success of new political groups, because that requires reconsidering the assumptions underlying our current economic and political system. Those who aren't convinced it's not just about racists and bigots can read the appendix first, "Beyond Identity Politics," as a starting point for the discussion of globalization and identity.

Lastly, I am an American citizen, having been born and raised in the United States, although I have now lived principally in Europe for many years. When I offer criticism of the European Union, people often suggest that of course an American will be against the EU, because a stronger Europe is a threat to the United States. I deal with this alleged conflict in the section "United States vs. Europe?", by addressing the problem through a different lens, one that sees the elites on both sides of the Atlantic as partners in the same failed vision. The populist revolt offers an opportunity to step back and assess the situation, breaking through the distorted view fed by fear of questioning one's own beliefs. My request is simply that you consider the arguments I present on their merits, avoiding excuses that could be used to minimize their import, as well as the temptation to blame the messenger for an unwelcome truth. I come not to bury Europe, but to suggest a way for the transatlantic community to make up for its dangerous errors of the past 40 years.

Andrew Spannaus, March 27, 2019

INTRODUCTION

In 2016, the world began to change. The march of globalization, trumpeting the disappearance of physical and economic borders, was stopped in its tracks, blocked by a series of political events that marked the beginning of the end of an era. The two major events that shocked the world that year were Brexit, when the voters of the United Kingdom chose to leave the European Union, and the election of Donald Trump to the Presidency of the United States, after a campaign in which the country's political and financial elites were targeted as never before in recent history.

In both cases, there was a revolt of the voters, an insurrection of "regular people" against the structures of political and media power, that upset the political balance of two of the leading countries of the Western world. And the revolt didn't stop there: it continued in 2017 and 2018 with a series of elections across continental Europe, with the growth of protest movements and candidates willing to challenge a system that until recently seemed impossible to change. Under attack was the European Union and the notion that governance is now supranational, and thus national interests should longer exist. From France to Germany to Italy, recent elections have rewarded politicians and political parties who have embraced criticism of globalization and the anti-establishment message that has been so effective in the United States as well.

Any practical changes as a result of this populist wave in Europe are still limited. The EU institutions are working hard to defend themselves against those who criticize supranational bodies as the main source of difficulties for middle and lower-class citizens. The most evident changes so far have been the turmoil over Brexit, and the formation of the new Italian government in June 2018, a coalition between two anti-establishment parties, the Five-Star Movement (M5S) and the League. Other than that, the populists have generally fallen short of their goals.

In the Netherlands, the Freedom Party of Geert Wilders did worse than expected in the elections of March 2017, receiving only 13% of the votes. In the first round of the French presidential elections, in April 2017, the two "extreme" candidates, Marine Le Pen on the right and Jean-Luc Mélenchon on the left, combined to receive 40% of the votes; but in the run-off two weeks later Le Pen was defeated decisively by Emmanuel Macron. In the September 2017 German elections, the anti-EU party Alternative for Germany increased its national vote total to over 12%, exceeding 20% in some regions; while the party's growth has had an effect on the balance between the other major parties, it has no role in governing the country.

The countries where parties considered to be populist and critical of the European Union have achieved power are Austria and Italy. In the former, the Freedom Party (FPO) came in third in the October 2018 elections with 26% of the vote, and is now in a governing coalition with the conservative Austrian People's Party. In the Italian elections on March 4, 2018, the Five-Star Movement came in first by a long shot with 32% of the vote. The League was third with 17%, a huge increase over its past national totals, which ultimately allowed it to form a coalition government with the M5S.

The government of Viktor Orban in Hungary is also often grouped in with the populists of the countries of Western Europe. The policy prescriptions are similar in some areas, such as the anti-immigrant rhetoric, but Orban's path to power was more traditional, as he emerged from an existing political coalition. Most anti-establishment movements in Western Europe, on the other hand, have attacked mainstream parties from the outside, rather than allying with established forces. This Eastern European form of populism thus has different characteristics, although it also plays an important role in the challenge to the power of the European Union.

Target: the EU

What does this mean for Europe as a common political entity? The right-wing populists generally take a hard line on immigration, an issue they have used effectively to grow their support. However, what scares the elites most, as we will see, is that almost all of the anti-establishment parties have been heavily critical of the economic policies of the European Union, especially the single currency, the Euro.

In Italy, both the M5S and League previously called for the country to leave the Euro, although both backtracked under institutional pressure once in office. Yet the new Italian government quickly clashed with the European Commission (EC) over economic policy, with Rome aiming to stimulate the economy by raising social spending and lowering taxes, which means running afoul of the budget criteria set by European treaties and regulations. The EC fought hard to hold the line, demanding Italy stay on the path towards a balanced budget, but ultimately ceded some ground in a compromise. In essence, a higher deficit in the short-term was exchanged for heavy costs to be triggered in future fiscal years, such as tax hikes and freezing pensions, unless new resources are found to cover the gap..

On the budgetary question and other issues, the authority of the EU institutions seems to be only slightly weakened at this time. Italy failed to get significant support from other European governments in its budget battle, but few of those governments are directly influenced by the Euroskeptic factions in their respective countries. The European Parliamentary elections to be held at the end of May 2019 promise to be a turning point, however. The question of EU policy will be squarely on the table, and Euroskeptic parties are expected to considerably increase their vote totals. If they were to reach a majority in the European Parliament, the prospects for further integration, or even maintaining the current level of integration, would be grim.

Even if Euroskeptics do not reach a majority, though, the European Parliament will soon more accurately reflect the current opinions of citizens around the continent – with considerable percentages being skeptical towards the EU – making it harder to move forward with plans that do not have popular support. This is true despite the fact that the Parliament has relatively little power compared to the Commission and the Council, which de facto set the Union's overall political direction. Critics of greater integration will no longer be relegated to a small minority, unable to make their voices heard; the battle over the future of Europe will be out in the open, and the population will be more involved. This is the last thing the supporters of European integration wanted to see, but frankly, they should have seen it coming.

The austerity policies implemented starting in 2010, in countries such as Greece, Spain and Italy, provoked a strong public reaction within a short period of time. Voters turned to political forces that railed against the establishment and called into question the legitimacy of the European Union. However, rather than taking a serious look in the mirror to address the emerging dissent, the political class across Europe attempted to minimize the problem. With the help of an obliging media, the anti-system sentiment was branded as a primitive reaction by people who refuse to join the new world, the world of globalization in which old certainties are called into question. The desire for a stable job, worries about a loss of cultural values or the transfer of power from politicians to financial markets, have often been classified as elements of a futile quest to turn back time. If people are upset with the leaders or bureaucrats in Brussels, it is simply because they have not yet accepted the new reality: that is the view in the halls of power. A majority of politicians still believe that the disruption brought by globalization, including downward pressure on living standards, is too deep to be overturned, and sooner or later everyone will have to adapt.

The "people" have other ideas. Given the opportunity to express their views through a democratic vote, the citizens of numerous Western countries have sent a strong message of protest, rejecting the inevitability of a model based on neoliberal economics and the disappearance of borders, and throwing their support to candidates who are populists and at times demagogues. The calls for moderation and civility have been futile. People who are mad at their politicians and who don't trust the mass media simply get madder when they are branded as ignorant, racist, and reactionary. There certainly are individuals and groups who meet this description, but the recent electoral shocks have been driven largely by socio-economic discontent. This is the context of the revolt of the voters, from the election results over the past two years, to the repercussions that could be seen in the near future.

The greatest danger

Can the Western liberal establishment survive this revolt? Can the European Union continue its path of integration, or is it destined to take a step backwards from the consolidation of supranational institutions? The attitude among the elites of closing ranks, of "resisting" against the protest and denying its justification, is the greatest danger for the future of the transatlantic world. The discontent has arisen for good reasons, and the only way to prevent the most worrying elements of populism from increasing their influence is to address the problem at the root. A profound revision of the policies of the past thirty years is needed, in particular on the economic front, before the situation gets out of control.

The complaints of a laborer who has lost his job, of a temporary worker who is unable to maintain her family, or a young person who is pessimistic about his future, have common roots: the loss of power by national political institutions, and the consequent destruction of the productive economy through the growing weight of power of supranational financial interests that favor short-term gain over long-term growth. The problem also goes beyond the implications of the political protests that represent a threat to the current ruling class, to touch the role of the West with respect to the world as a whole. The decline of the West's real power, due to the shift away from industry and productive investment, has affected the calculus of how to deal with new global players, such as China. This is yet another reason why the West would do better to attempt to maintain its leading economic role, rather than shoot itself in the foot with anti-industrial and anti-social policies, becoming weaker both internally and externally.

In this book I will analyze not only the recent, tangible problems that have caused the current political upheaval, but also the longer-term processes behind the growing divide between the population and the governing class. I will look at the role of the nation-state and the attempts to supersede it by a globalist elite.[1] And I will examine the reasons for the creation of the European Union, a structure founded as an instrument to maintain peace among European nations, that was subsequently transformed into a supranational body with the aim of eliminating the national sovereignty of its Member States. I will ask whether it is worthwhile, and possible, to continue with the construction of a superstate, or whether it is necessary to take a step backwards, while still maintaining forms of collaboration between participating nations. The most pressing issue is how the very existence of the European Union is called into question by the popular protests across

---

1   The world "globalist" is used here to refer to the ideology which considers nation-states to be obsolete, and thus advocates the elimination of barriers between countries, based on the notion that national interests should give way to a globally shared set of values. The attempt by certain media outlets to brand the word "globalist" as inherently racist, is precisely an example of the problem being discussed, i.e. attempting to exclude discussion of a real issue by concentrating only on its most negative characteristics, cutting off debate and deepening the gap between opposing views.

the Western world. Lastly, I will indicate the path towards a return to policies that can provide peace and prosperity in Europe and in the West as a whole, based on the principles that generated progress in the past. And I will show that, for too long, those principles have been ignored, poorly applied and often distorted for aims that have nothing to do with the good of the population.

PART I
THE STRENGTH OF ECONOMIC POPULISM

FERTILE GROUND

The Brexit vote in the United Kingdom, and the election of Donald Trump in the United States, in 2016, were the events that many consider to mark the start of the populist revolt that then spread across continental Europe in 2017 and 2018. The reasons behind these events were actually quite evident, but simply ignored for decades by politicians who thought that voters did not have any real alternatives to mainstream policies. Starting in the early 1970s, a process began in which the financial economy increasingly dominated the real economy. Through a series of shocks and legislative changes in leading countries, from the abandonment of fixed exchange rates in 1971 to the deregulation policies initiated in the UK and the U.S. in the 1980s, it became easier for financial interests to make money at the expense of the real economy. The result was a push for immediate profits, to the detriment of stable investment.

The decision by the Nixon administration to float the dollar, on August 15, 1971, made it more difficult to plan investments and international trade in the mid- and long-term. If the exchange rate between the currencies of country A and country B can change by 5%, or even 50%, within just a few months or years, there is a clear risk in committing money for economic projects, even if only for the purchase of materials or products abroad.

The result of the end of the Bretton Woods currency system was the gradual financialization of the economy, i.e. the growth of the financial operations used to offset the instability created by a world without stable exchange rates. Today, to make any international investment, it is mandatory to purchase a sort of insurance policy, in the form of financial derivatives. Derivatives are useful to hedge against risks, but starting in the 1990s, a situation was created in which the speculative component of these instruments became dominant. Finance is no longer an accessory to the real economy, but now moves 15 or even 20 times the amount of global GDP. Thus, assets such as oil, food, and currencies are bought and sold continuously by traders who are not interested in actually using them, but only profiting from short-term price variations. Capital moves rapidly and bubbles are created and burst, often with devastating effects on the real economy, which requires stability to function.

Finance has always had a role, of course, and speculative bubbles have often led to crashes and depressions in various periods of history. The characteristic of the shift in the Western world over the past half-century is that of a structural change that has provoked not one, but many crises. "Financial innovation" has de facto been treated as the main driver of growth, as political institutions have adopted the view that bolstering the financial markets translates into an improvement of the economy in general. An obvious example of the failure of this approach is the growth of speculative instruments created to trade mortgages in the United States, which had little to do with encouraging sustainable home ownership, and much to do with finding a new stream of liquidity to drive activity on the capital markets. The result was the catastrophic 2008 crash that affected the world economy as a whole.

Precious little has been done to address this structural change. Policymakers have focused on guaranteeing the stability of financial markets, and thus protecting returns for those who invest in them. The maximization of "shareholder value" through the search for efficiency has translated into driving down wages and benefits for workers, on the one hand, and to the definitive loss of well-paying manufacturing jobs, due to outsourcing to cheap-labor countries, in many others.[1] Over the long-term, there has been a well-documented increase in inequality,[2]

---

1   For many years, there have been attempts to play down the loss of manufacturing jobs in the U.S. due to outsourcing to cheap labor countries; the argument has been that technology is actually the main culprit. For a concise explanation of the problems with this line of thought, see: Jeffry Bartash, 'China really is to blame for millions of lost U.S. manufacturing jobs, new study finds', *MarketWatch*, May 14, 2018. The article cites research by David Autor of MIT, among others, on the crumbling consensus for the technology argument, which I also cited here in a 2017 article for the Aspen Institute: Andrew Spannaus, 'Tariffs and standards: Towards a new trade policy' *Aspenia online*, February 16, 2017.

2   See, for example, the "Inequality" page of the Organisation for Economic Cooperation and Development's website, which begins as follows: *"Income inequality in OECD countries is at its highest level for the past half century. The average income of the richest 10% of the population is about nine times that of the poorest 10% across the OECD, up from seven times 25 years ago."*

interlinked with a gradual decrease in purchasing power and living standards for the many.[3] This doesn't mean that people don't have more *stuff* nowadays, due to new digital technologies for example, but most have to work more, with more uncertainty, to make a decent living. The percentage of the poor and destitute is actually higher today in the U.S. than it was 50 years ago,[4] for example, but at the same time there has been a considerable increase in the ranks of the super-rich.

The mechanisms of the financial economy have brought profound change in the international political sphere as well. Speculative movements have become a form of pressure under which countries can be brought to their knees, as national governments are no longer able to protect their own citizens' interests in the face of a financial attack. Some might say that in the long run the markets are generally right, i.e. capital movements tend to reward or punish countries based on the quality of their economic policies. This ideological, tautological position is easily unmasked with reference to any number of financial crises, from the attacks on the British pound and Italian lira in 1992, forcing them out of the European Rate Mechanism, to a series of crises in the 1990s and beyond affecting countries such as Mexico, Thailand, Russia and Argentina. In such cases, speculative capital was used not in the interest of actual economic activity, but only to make a quick buck, exploiting misperceptions in a way that led to disastrous contractions in living standards for the respective populations.

The problem is not the existence of financial markets per se, but rather the outsized role they have been given in determining economic policy. In a free economy, investors have the right to seek profit, but what's good for the markets is not necessarily good for the economy as a whole.

---

3   On the stagnation of real wages, see Drew Desilver, 'For most U.S. workers, real wages have barely budged in decades,' *Pew Research Center*, August 7, 2018.
    On the decline in purchasing power, see the "Purchasing Power" page on www.Investopedia.com, which explains: *"One way to think about purchasing power is to imagine if you made the same salary as your grandfather 40 years ago. Today you would need a much greater salary just to maintain the same quality of living. By the same token, a homebuyer looking for homes 10 years ago in the $300,000 to 350,000 price range had more options to consider than people have now."*

4   See 'What is the current poverty rate in the United States?', *Center for Poverty Research, University of California, Davis*. Updated October 15, 2018.

Economics and identity

The economic discontent produced by this process has now boiled over; and the opposition goes beyond merely a question of people's paychecks, to encompass the identity of communities and entire countries. Areas such as the Midwest of the United States, or sectors such as steel and textiles in Europe, have seen dramatic changes over the past few decades, leading to a shift in how people see their own roles in the national, and global, economy. The diminishment of the "productive identity" of an American farmer, or a European manufacturing worker, is a factor that cannot be ignored.

To tell someone it doesn't matter where products are made, as long as prices stay low, is a blow to the view Western countries have developed of themselves since World War II. There is of course no law of physics or economics which says that people shouldn't change what they do; technological and social revolutions are quite common in history. Yet in the case of globalization there is no denying that many changes have been due not to some inevitable process of upheaval ultimately leading to progress. Numerous Western industries have been uprooted in order to exploit weak labor and environmental regulations in countries that were desperate for investment. Political decisions were made to further this process, disregarding the long-term effects they would have on the workforce in developed nations. The defenders of globalization say that people have to be ready to adapt, yet when adaptation means seeing a worsening of one's standard of living, accompanied by a loss of social cohesion, it's not surprising that frustration and discontent grow over time.

For example: immigration

One of the major issues that has emerged in recent years is, of course, immigration. A strong reaction has developed among conservatives in particular, but has expanded to have a general impact far beyond those who could be considered xenophobic or racist. In many countries, right-wing populists have used immigration as one of their major issues in criticizing globalization. The notion that the disappearance of borders means that people should be able to go wherever they wish, has fed into fears of a rapid change in the identity of Western European countries in particular, in both economic and social terms.

There is no denying the centrality of the issue of immigration, yet it is political malpractice not to recognize how it is linked to the overall reaction to globalization, starting in the economic sphere. The insecurity that people feel, due to difficulty in making ends meet, feeds a fear of immigrants, who are seen as a threat to economic well-being. If immigrants are willing to accept lower pay and less comfortable living conditions, it is not hard to see how that could put downward pressure on the living standards of others. Donald Trump used this point to great effect in 2016, as his rhetoric on immigration was (and is) closely linked to the economic difficulties of the middle class. His campaign website invoked the need to stop immigration from Mexico due to "unfair economic subsidies" that have "eliminated thousands of American jobs." The wall, he claimed, would lead to "economic and income gains due to an increase in production in the United States".[5]

Tying anti-immigrant proposals to economic decline does not absolve Trump or others of responsibility for unnecessarily fomenting further social divisions. However, it is essential to recognize that economic conditions provide fertile ground for such inflammatory rhetoric. Academic research backs up this correlation, finding that economic difficulties can feed racism. In 2014, researchers at New York University determined that people's physical perception of skin color actually varied in relation to the scarcity of economic resources. Their conclusion was that "perceived scarcity influences people's visual representations of race in a way that may promote discrimination".[6]

It is also not surprising that during a crisis, support increases for more extreme political forces. Academic research in Europe has documented this link going all the way back to 1870, by analyzing the political history of twenty different democratic countries.[7] German researchers found that the crisis of 2008 inaugurated a period in which support grew strongly for right-wing parties, along with a general increase of protests and violence. The conclusion is elementary, and intuitive: anti-immigrant attitudes grow and prosper when the population feels that their well-being is under attack.

---

5   Positions on Trump's 2016 campaign website, no longer online.
6   Amy R. Krosch, David M. Amodio, 'Economic scarcity alters the perception of race', *Proceedings of the National Academy of Sciences of the United States of America*, June 24, 2014 111 (25) 9079-9084.
7   M. Funke, M. Schularick, C. Trebesch, 'The political aftermath of financial crises: Going to extremes', *Vox* (2015).

Ignoring the signs of revolt

Now I would like to look at how the economic aspect of the populist revolt has been so central to the success of the anti-establishment movements across the transatlantic world in the past few years. The point is simple: either political institutions begin to deal seriously with the fundamental economic changes that have taken place over a period of decades, or nobody should expect the revolt of the voters to subside, with all of the negative side effects seen to this point. And there is no doubt things could get even worse, in Europe in particular, where the last instances of dictatorship and destruction of democratic institutions are not so far in the past.

On the heels of the global financial crisis that exploded in 2008, came the Euro crisis, a series of shocks that spread fears of default by several EU Member States. Bubbles burst, economies cratered, and national budgets went heavily into the red. The solution, according to the "Troika" – the name for the informal body created by the European Commission, the European Central Bank, and the International Monetary Fund – demanded that governments enact austerity in order to deal with the crisis. That is, the response to a drop in economic activity, which led to widespread loss of jobs and wealth for the population, was to cut government spending in order to avoid the growth of national debt.

It was a recipe for disaster: a pro-cyclical response based on the notion that the combination of a balanced budget and neoliberal policies such as privatization and liberalization would automatically create economic growth. The contrary was true. The harsh measures imposed on countries like Greece, Spain, and Italy caused deep recessions and a social welfare emergency due to cuts in investment and spending on services such as health care and pensions; while the "structural reforms" demanded by the the European Union generally meant more labor market flexibility, meaning favoring short-term and part-time employment, and turning over publicly-controlled assets to private interests. The EU institutions became the face of austerity and national humiliation. It should be no surprise that political rebellion soon followed.

Greece and Italy are the two clearest examples of a response of the voters to EU economic policies, before the series of elections kicked off by the Brexit vote in 2016. Starting in 2011, Greece was forced to sign multiple "memorandum" agreements with the Troika in order to guarantee repayment of its debt, requiring massive budget cuts, with devastating effects on the Greek population. The governments of Greece had certainly made mistakes, such as misrepresenting their accounts to ensure membership in the Euro – with the help of Goldman Sachs[8] – and tolerating corruption and tax evasion. Yet the cure imposed by the Troika was much worse than the disease. Poverty has doubled since 2008, reaching over 35% of the population in 2016, while foreign aid has mostly gone to repay the countries' creditors.

Politically, the result was the growth of a political party named Syriza, led by the young Alexis Tsipras. Syriza's key issue was opposition to austerity, heavily criticizing the accords with the Troika that continued to demand more "fiscal discipline." That ultimately led to the referendum called in July 2015 called by Tsipras – by then the Prime Minister – and his charismatic Finance Minister Yanis Varoufakis, on whether Greece should accept an additional memorandum entailing more austerity in order to pay off international creditors. The "no" vote was 62%, but Tsipras ultimately went against the wishes of his own people, signing the new memorandum due to fears of the reaction if Greece sought to leave the Euro.[9]

The Greek crisis, which initially emerged in 2009, was accompanied by increased worries about the financial stability of other European countries with considerable debt. One of these was Italy, which had never even come close to respecting the EU parameters on this point, having a debt-to-GDP ratio of over 120%, compared to the target of 60%. Although this debt was relatively stable and the Italian economy had mostly survived the effects of the 2008-2009 financial crisis due to its banks' low exposure to the speculative instruments that wreaked havoc elsewhere, Italy became the new target, and pressure built rapidly in mid-2011. The government of Silvio Berlusconi was forced to resign in November of that year, due to pressure from financial markets and political machinations led by German Chancellor Angela

---

8   See 'How Goldman Sachs Helped Greece to Mask its True Debt', *Spiegel Online*, February 8, 2010, and 'Greek debt crisis: Goldman Sachs could be sued for helping hide debts when it joined euro', *Independent*, July 11, 2015.

9   Former Greek Finance Minister Yanis Varoufakis told of the fears of a coup d'etat if Greece were to leave the Euro in his 2017 book: *Adults in the Room: My Battle With Europe's Deep Establishment* (Bodley Head, 2017).

Merkel and French President Nicolas Sarkozy.[10] Mario Monti, a professor of economics at the prestigious Bocconi University in Milan, was appointed as the next Prime Minister, beginning three years of austerity that would lead to a 7% drop in Italy's GDP.[11] The Italian population initially welcomed Monti's technocrats with open arms, but the honeymoon did not last long. When it became clear that the cure was worse than the disease, the political climate began to shift rapidly.

What happened in the Italian elections of 2013 should have been seen as an urgent alarm, but the governing class of Europe as a whole was apparently too obtuse to recognize what can now be clearly identified as a precursor to the populist revolt of 2016-2018. In the February 2013 campaign, the anti-establishment Five-Star Movement, organized on the Internet and through "meet-ups" among citizens, adopted the message of publicly telling off the "caste" of corrupt politicians and those around them who enriched themselves at the expense of the general population. Despite refusing to talk to the press or go on TV, the movement received 25% of the national vote; an earthquake which indicated the widespread rejection of the political institutions due to decades of policies that undermined the economic well-being and stability constructed in the postwar period.

A smart reaction to the Italian vote of 2013, and the Greek referendum of 2015, would have been to recognize that the austerity policies were provoking heightened anger directed at both national political leaders and the EU itself. Yet European institutions continued to exert heavy pressure on the offending countries, ultimately getting them to toe the fiscal responsibility line. The Greek government went ahead with

---

10   Merkel phoned Italian State President Giorgio Napolitano in October 2011, "urging him to nudge Berlusconi off the stage," "in order to save the Euro," according to press reports a few months later. See 'Merkel under fire over phone bid to oust Berlusconi', *Independent*, December 31, 2011, and 'Deepening Crisis Over Euro Pits Leader Against Leader', *Wall Street Journal*, December 30, 2011. There are reports claiming that Sarkozy was directly involved as well.

11   Some reject the notion that there really was austerity in Italy, since the overall state budget decreased only slightly. Whatever we want to call it, the fact is that taxes were increased, while social services and public investments were cut. The "savings" were meant to help reduce the deficit; this ended up being entirely useless, since the drop in economic growth ultimately produced more debt for the state, due, for example, to increased costs for social shock absorbers.

the memorandums, and the IMF, despite some limited self-criticism, continued to demand further budget cuts in order to pay off the debt. The governments that succeeded the technocrats in Italy spoke often about returning to growth over austerity, but failed to take the bold steps that could have led to a visible change. The result was that the EU budget orthodoxy remained in place, and became an easy target for the political movements that sought to channel the people's discontent. This took different forms in different countries, of course, but the European institutions were increasingly identified with policies that aggravated an already difficult situation for the middle and lower classes. Combined with the surge in immigration starting in 2014, storm clouds were forming on the horizon; but EU leaders continued to calmly insist that they were in control, and that things would get better if everyone just followed the rules, their rules.

THE VOTERS SPEAK: BREXIT AND TRUMP

Brexit

Much can be said about the internal situation in the United Kingdom before the Brexit referendum of June 23, 2016, but we should first recall the country's somewhat anomalous relationship with EU institutions. In 1946, Winston Churchill spoke of the need for a "United States of Europe," but did not foresee the participation of Britain, which, he said, already had its own grouping of nations, the Commonwealth. The UK joined the European Economic Community – but only in 1973, more than 15 years after its founding – and did not join the single currency. There has always been a level of distrust preventing a further transfer of sovereignty, resulting in a situation where the UK participates in European governance and the common market, but is not subject to the same monetary restrictions as other Member States.

In 2015, the pro-Leave parties exploited the immigration crisis created when numerous migrants massed across the English Channel in Calais, France, and attempted to smuggle themselves into the UK. It was the campaign led by Nigel Farage and the UKIP party, demanding a return to full sovereignty in part in order to deal with the immigration question, that pushed Prime Minister David Cameron to call the referendum. The idea was that most of the political world would support Remain, and thus the position trumpeted by Farage would be marginalized.

Yet the debate developed differently. Supporters of Leave began to concentrate on fiscal and economic questions, creating a debate on how much the EU costs the UK. Distortions were presented and mistakes were made, but the ultimate effect was that Leave gained votes. It is common to hear that this result was due to lies and superficial judgments, but the fact is that, as happened in the U.S. elections a few months later, in order for such arguments to take hold, there has to be fertile ground. That came from the effects of globalization and the austerity policies implemented by the Cameron government, which had impoverished certain segments of the population.

It is not hard to convince others in Europe that anti-immigrant views are endemic in the UK. Here too, however, it is important to recognize how economic conditions affect popular sentiment – as already documented above (see footnote 7) – causing people to lose their sense of solidarity. The battle over Brexit thus became a clash between different sectors of society. While urban areas generally voted heavily for Remain, more rural and poorer areas saw Leave dominate. The gap was identified by some as the difference between those who are well-off, and those who aren't. "If you've got money, you vote in... if you haven't got money, you vote out," was the view given by a Brexit supporter to journalist John Harris of *The Guardian* just before the vote.

Harris had travelled through the economically depressed areas of the United Kingdom, talking to people who in the past had voted for Labour, but had shifted to UKIP, citing the neoliberal bent adopted by Prime Minister Tony Blair in the 1990s. Immigration was not the only important issue: outsourcing, the difficulty of maintaining a decent standard of living, and cuts to social services were identified with the political class that ignored people's problems, and was now mobilizing to Remain.

Harris wrote:

> Brexit is the consequence of the economic bargain struck in the early 1980s, whereby we waved goodbye to the security and certainties of the postwar settlement, and were given instead an economic model that has just about served the most populous parts of the country, while leaving too much of the rest to anxiously decline.[1]

Some of these effects were aggravated in the period immediately preceding Brexit, thanks to welfare cuts implemented by the Cameron government in 2015 and 2016. One year before the vote, *The Guardian* had already written that austerity had "helped to

---

1   John Harris, 'If you've got money, you vote in... if you haven't got money, you vote out', *The Guardian*, June 24, 2016.

push hundreds of thousands of people below the breadline."[2] Just days before the vote itself, newspaper headlines read "UK poverty levels rise for first time in nearly a decade."[3] In explaining the role of neoliberalism in bolstering xenophobic sentiment, Ben Norton of *Salon* noted that "things are getting worse, not better, and everyone recognizes it".[4] It was easy for the supporters of Leave to exploit this situation to their benefit.

Trump beats expectations

The next major shock was, of course, the election of Donald Trump to the United States presidency. Since this book focuses on Europe, I will touch only briefly on some central points to be remembered, as they bear upon the discussion of the economic factors driving the revolt of the voters. There are many lessons to learn from the results of the 2016 elections in the U.S., but a key takeaway is to recognize the fallacy of the assumption that certain ethnic or social groups always vote the same way. The polls were relatively accurate compared to 2012, but a mistake was made: relying on Latinos, African-Americans, or women voters to reject Trump completely because of his offensive comments about them turned out to be a false assumption. Counting on an "identity" vote did not work, as Clinton ended up receiving a lower share of the vote than Obama did four years earlier in each case.

There has been a lot of talk about "angry white males," but Clinton got 66% of the Latino vote compared to 71% for Obama; and 88% of the African-American vote compared to 93% for Obama. The latter may seem easy to explain based on skin color, but this too would be a mistake based on "identity." In 1965, Lyndon Johnson got even more than Obama: 94% of the African-American vote, due to his commitment to the battle for civil rights. Even among women, Clinton lost a percentage point compared to 2012, taking 54% compared to Obama's 55% four years earlier.

2　Patrick Butler, 'Poverty – and child poverty in particular – is rising', *The Guardian*, April 29, 2015.

3　Jamie Micklethwaite, 'UK poverty levels rise for first time in nearly a decade', *EveningStandard*, June 28, 2016.

4　Ben Norton, 'How neoliberalism fuels the racist xenophobia behind Brexit and Donald Trump', *Salon*, July 1, 2016.

The crucial area of the country for Trump's election, though, was the Rust Belt, Midwestern states that have lost thousands of factories in recent decades, with the resulting economic difficulties for middle class families. Trump concentrated heavily on this area, with harsh attacks on globalization and trade deals, while trumpeting his message of bringing manufacturing jobs back to America.

It worked. Trump's wins in Michigan, Wisconsin, and Pennsylvania were essential to his election, and in each of these states he won by less than a single percentage point. The bellwether was the vote of union households. While Clinton famously took the first two of these states for granted, failing to go to Wisconsin even once during the campaign, a shift occurred in the labor vote that proved catastrophic for the Democrats. Among union voters Trump received 43% support, an improvement over the 40% that went to Mitt Romney four years earlier. On the Democratic side the shift was larger: while in 2012 Obama got 58% among union voters, Clinton went all the way down to 51%. Summing these two figures – which reflect a non-negligible shift of votes to third-party candidates as well – we see that the Democratic advantage among union voters was cut in half in the 2016 election.

Did Trump win, or did Clinton lose? It really doesn't matter. Trump received a minority of the popular vote, both nationally and in many key states, since third party candidates such as Gary Johnson (Libertarian) and Jill Stein (Green) pulled noticeable support. Whether people voted for Trump, against Clinton, for other candidates, or stayed home, the point is that the candidate most identified with the establishment was punished; an establishment seen as having pursued its own interests and not that of the majority of the people in certain areas of the country. Denying this reality is merely a recipe for deepening the political and social divide that has emerged so forcefully since 2016.

THE REVOLT IN EUROPE

The political movements and parties that garnered increased attention, and votes, across Europe in 2017 and 2018, share one position in particular: criticism of the European Union. Figures such as Geert Wilders in the Netherlands are known for their anti-Islam and anti-immigrant positions, but at the same time movements have sprouted up in Greece, Spain, and Italy that are not based on identity or racial division. Rather they draw on people's anger due to the social effects of the economic crisis and the austerity measures imposed by the European Union. As in the cases of Brexit and the election of Donald Trump, the critical mass for success of the populist movements around Europe is reached only when their spokesmen are smart enough to focus on a strong critique of the economic elites, and the difficulties created for the middle class.

The irony is that the attitude of mainstream politicians and media has contributed greatly to the success of the populists. For years criticism of the EU was considered unacceptable, and identified with "extreme" parties assumed to be anti-democratic or racist. It was a poor attempt to shield European institutions from criticism, and it backfired. Not only did skepticism of the EU grow, but a huge void was left in the political debate, which populist parties rapidly filled.

The Netherlands

One case that shows how parties already identified as populist before recent times have shifted their message to tap into the anti-EU sentiment, is that of the Freedom Party (PVV) in the Netherlands. The party's leader, Geert Wilders, is known in particular for his anti-Islam position. The PVV's election campaign in 2017 was indeed focused on the "de-Islamization" of the Netherlands, but the party also adopted the position of "Nexit," i.e. that the Netherlands should leave the European Union. And despite the fact that Wilders claims to be a follower of former British Prime Minister Margaret Thatcher, his program had many points that went in quite a different direction on economic policy: the abolition of co-pays for health care services, the reduction of the minimum retirement age to 65, and the defense of public funds for assistance to the elderly. Wilders also strongly attacked budget cuts, accusing the previous government of having "destroyed our country with its austerity policies."

Wilders' pro-social spending platform was a transparent attempt to exploit the type of economic discontent that has spread across the Western world. It didn't quite work. His continued focus on immigrants and the defense of national identity made it clear where his priorities were, and outgoing Prime Minister Mark Rutte succeeded in outflanking him on the question of Islam – conveniently picking a public fight with the Turkish government over its attempts to influence Dutch politics. Along with other tactical mistakes, the PVV ended up falling short of its goal, despite increasing its national vote total to 13.1%. Wilders didn't convince many people that he was their economic champion, but his attempt to exploit the political revolt against austerity is indicative of what other parties around Europe have done with greater success.

France

A country where the merger between nationalist politics and the reaction against the neoliberal policies of the European Union was more effective is France. The founder of the far-right party *Front National*, Jean-Marie Le Pen, was known for his strong defense of national identity, along with often provocative and racist comments. His daughter Marine, on the other hand, attempted to soften her tone on immigration, and raise it more with regard to the EU.

The growth of the *Front National* (FN) was due not only to the shift in leadership to a partially more palatable leader; France has also suffered from the effects of economic and financial globalization, with growing inequality and a declining middle class. Thus the French population, which already has a strong nationalist sentiment, was naturally receptive to a critique of European economic policy.

When she presented her candidacy in Lyon on February 5, 2017, Le Pen railed against "our leaders who have chosen deregulated globalization," presenting herself as the alternative to both the right and the left that are dominated by what the FN calls the "tyrannical system" of the EU. She also charged that immigration had paralyzed the economy and provoked mass unemployment.

What is interesting is that the FN's invective was not merely superficial bombast, but actually identified a path for changes in the current economic and financial architecture. The first change it proposed was to leave the Euro – a common refrain among populists – but not to return to a floating exchange rate system in which the value of currencies can be determined by speculative transactions on the financial markets. This is an important point, because it suggests a restoration of national sovereignty while avoiding the threat of financial instability that emerged gradually since the abandonment of fixed exchange rates in 1971 (as discussed in Chapter 1 – Fertile Ground)

Le Pen's proposal was to return to the European Monetary System (EMS), created in the 1970s in the aftermath of the end of the Bretton Woods fixed exchange rates, resuming use of the European Currency Unit as a unit of account to settle payments among nations. This is not a popular position among economists today, as the common currency has become a dogma to be defended at all costs, and objectively, it would be complex and difficult to attempt to unwind it. The EMS system also wasn't perfect, ultimately being taken down by speculation – or better, by the failure of European governments to combat that speculation – in 1992. Yet this proposal encouraged a debate on how to take a step back towards monetary sovereignty, without abandoning cooperation between European nations.

The second interesting proposal brought up by the FN was the elimination of the independence of central banks, and thus a return to a national bank in France. This is also a taboo for most current experts, as it reflects the goal of restoring the role of the state in economic policy. In addition to influencing interest rates, a key point would be the management of the public debt, neutralizing the pressure financial speculation currently puts on governments through the secondary bond market.

The same point has been raised recently by leading members of the government of Italy, a country which has suffered considerably from speculation against its debt in recent years. The proposal, supported, for example, by Paolo Savona, a former government minister and now head of Italy's financial market authority, is to reverse what is known as the "divorce" between the Italian Treasury and the Bank of Italy of

1981. Before that, the Bank acted as the buyer of last resort for Treasury bonds, alleviating speculative pressure. Once this backstop was gone, interest rates were determined by the market, leading the public debt to almost double in just a decade.[1] Today neoliberal economists and EU bureaucrats demand that Italy slash its budget in order to reduce the debt. It never works, as cuts in investment actually end up hurting the economy and ultimately increase the relative weight of the debt, but almost nobody dares mention how the bulk of that debt came about.

The irony is that in an attempt to stimulate European economies, the ECB began to purchase a considerable quantity of state bonds on the market in March 2015. For countries such as Italy and Spain, the operation acted as a backstop that contributed to the reduction of interest rates, with billions in public savings. Thus, a by-product of the European Central Bank's operations to provide liquidity to the financial markets was performing the function that national banks used to perform regarding the public debt. Rather than recognizing the essential nature of public intervention, though, and institutionalizing it, those "extraordinary" measures were subsequently wound down, and the idea of the ECB guaranteeing the public debt of European countries now seems essentially impossible given the current divisions. This situation shows the no-man's land in which EU governance finds itself: nations have been stripped of essential powers, but the supranational institutions are unable, or unwilling, to wield those powers to protect the interests of the Member States.

The growth of the right-wing *Front National* was not the only expression of the populist revolt in the French elections of 2017; on the left, the former socialist Jean-Luc Mélenchon also rode an anti-globalization message to a strong showing in the first round, with 19%, just a few points behind Le Pen and Emmanuel Macron, who advanced to the run-off. With his new party *La France Insoumise* (Unsubmissive France), Mélenchon was heavily critical of the EU, although he did not call for exiting the Euro, and campaigned on a significant increase in social spending and state intervention into the economy. He was not a

---

1   In 1980, Italy's public debt was 55% of GDP. By 1990, it had reached 95%, to then rise to 120% only a few years later. At the same time, public spending increased by only 1% of GDP in the decade of the 1980s. These figures give the lie to the notion that the debt was due to the country "living beyond its means" through out-of-control government expenditures.

true outsider, having been part of the French political system for years, but his campaign showed the strength of left-wing populism as well, without the anti-immigrant and anti-Islam orientation of many other protest parties.

Macron's victory in the presidential run-off was hailed by many as the salvation of Europe, as he defended the EU strongly against Le Pen's attacks. The pro-EU faction around Europe played up this point, hoping to rapidly forget that over 40% of French voters had supported candidates heavily critical of the EU in the first round. Yet the reality was that although Marine Le Pen is more palatable than her father, the extreme positions her party has represented for years are still too much for the majority of the French. People rejected the FN's rhetoric, but it didn't take long for the view of Macron as the savior of Europe to come crashing down. Less than a year after his election, the French President found himself facing the revolt of the "Yellow Vests," who repeatedly occupied the streets of Paris to protest against difficult living conditions for the middle class outside of large cities. At the same time, Macron lost numerous members of his government, and his approval ratings sunk into the 20s. The shiny new object who was supposed to stop populism crashed pretty quickly.

Germany

The voters of the most prosperous and stable large country in Europe, Germany, went to the polls in September 2017. Despite an initial surge by the Social Democrats (SPD), as the election approached the consensus around the continent was that Chancellor Angela Merkel would easily win a fourth term, allowing her to tie the record set by Helmut Kohl. But things did not go exactly as expected.

In the September 24 elections, the two largest parties, the Christian Democrats (CDU/CSU) and the Social Democrats, both got less support than anticipated, while the populists of Alternative for Germany (AfD) got more. In absolute terms, the Christian Democrats lost over 8%, while the Social Democrats lost 5%. The AfD made it up to 12.6%. The end result was a situation in which the CDU/CSU and the SPD were forced to once again form a coalition government – going back on the SPD's promise before the vote not to do so – in order to keep the AfD out of power.

For years, the narrative in Europe has been that Germany is so strong economically, and has managed labor issues and the internal imbalance between West and East so well, that there was little to worry about in terms of political protest. If anything, the opposition to the EU stemmed from resistance to pooling the country's wealth with the perceived deadbeats of Southern Europe, that were resisting rigorous budget rules and the hard work needed to build an efficient economy.

The reality, however, was a bit different. While Germany is certainly the strongest economy in Europe, the way it got there in the past 30 years has been far from ideal. In the 1990s, the neoliberal "shock therapy" applied to the former German Democratic Republic caused widespread unemployment and poverty in the East, where socio-economic conditions are still markedly worse than in the West. At the same time, Western businesses gained millions of new consumers and low-cost suppliers from the East, such that the supposed cost of reunification actually represented a massive stimulus for Western German industry.[2]

Germany has had another "advantage" in the past 20 years. The benefits of productivity gains have not been transferred to the labor force. One of the key components of this process is the "Hartz IV" reform enacted in 2005, which forces the unemployed to work for just a few Euros an hour in order to maintain limited social benefits. This "labor market flexibility" – one of the central goals of the "structural reforms" constantly demanded by the EU – has certainly helped German industry, which has benefitted from low-cost, highly flexible work. What was surprising, was that this situation did not seem to have provoked much opposition among the population. In the 2017 elections, a change became evident.

There are, in fact, entire areas in Germany known as "Hartz IV neighborhoods," in the periphery of large cities. And the number of working poor in the country is close to 10%.[3] Just as in the rest of the West, wealth in Germany is stratified, and the conditions are present for a protest against the governing class whose policies have made life more difficult for many.

The AfD was founded in 2013 in opposition to the policies of the European Union, calling for a return to national sovereignty and the

---

2   The details of this process are presented very clearly in the 2013 book by Italian author Vladimiro Giacché, *Anschluss. L'annessione. L'unificazione della Germania e il futuro dell'Europa* (Reggio Emilia: Imprimatur, 2013).

3   Eurostat data elaborated by Prometeia

abandonment of the Euro, along with strongly conservative social positions. In the 2014 elections the party received 7% of the vote nationally, but in the regional elections of 2016, it got well over 20% in eastern regions such as Saxony-Anhalt and Mecklenburg-Pomerania. Its vote total in the 2017 elections showed that Germany is not immune to the populist protest.

In Germany, opposition to the EU is not the same as in countries which have suffered through the austerity policies of recent years. There is a considerable portion of the population that, in addition to fearing immigration and terrorism, feels no obligation to pitch in to help countries that are less efficient; thus, they resist greater integration at the European level.

There is some unjustified arrogance in this attitude, but also some reality. The economic recipes of the Troika, like those of the International Monetary Fund for the countries of Africa and Latin America, have completely failed to resolve the economic problems of EU member states. In the best-case scenarios, the costs of the crisis have been shifted to the weaker parts of the population; in the worst, austerity has led to a collapse of economic activity and a disastrous increase in poverty.

When a German citizen is told that assistance must be provided to other countries, it's not hard to see why opposition arises. The measures taken simply don't work, so there will always be more to pay in the future. The problem is that political leaders have been far from honest on this point, not only failing to explain the effects of the neoliberal policies, but also concealing the fact that "assistance" often returns to the donor countries in the form of repayment of bank loans; this is what happened with the so-called rescue packages for Greece, in which hundreds of billions of Euros actually went to avoid catastrophic losses for German and French banks, not to the Greeks.

So while the Germans get mad about paying for others, European governments are actually working to guarantee the profits of their banks. And at the same time, social difficulties increase in the wealthy countries as well. Overall, this situation shifts attention from the real problems, and foments division among countries based on false perceptions. For years German, Italian, and French citizens knew little about how these mechanisms worked, and thus failed to properly identify those responsible. Today, the situation is somewhat different, as the populist movements have pointed the finger at the EU institutions which have promoted an economic model that simply hasn't worked, perpetuating social problems and divisions across the continent. That is not to say that there is some sort of continental "awakening" and alliance among peoples, but it is harder now to hide the mistakes made in recent years, and failure to change those policies is becoming decidedly more risky.

Italy

The considerable anti-establishment sentiment that exploded in Italy in the 2013 elections – referenced at the beginning of this book – took a decisive step forward in 2018. The Five-Star Movement had received 25% of the vote in its first national election, and thus had a large number of parliamentarians. The other major parties, however, had no intention of allowing them to share power, and major media continued to take every opportunity to denigrate the M5S. The newcomers had plenty of faults, from a lack of experience and competence, to conflicting ideas on some points, but it was a grave mistake to try to write them off as some sort of short-term phenomenon, which "serious people" shouldn't consider. To anyone who had a clear understanding of the broader socio-economic situation, the M5S's anti-corruption, pro-social spending positions seemed likely, if anything, to gain more support, given the refusal of the mainstream political class to take decisive measures to change the trajectory of the country.[4]

The Italian elections of March 4, 2018 were an earthquake, as for the first time a populist party was the outright winner, and by a long shot. The M5S got 32% of the vote, well beyond the total for the second place finisher, the Democratic Party (PD) led by former Prime Minister Matteo Renzi, which came in at 18%. That was a huge fall for the PD, considering its results of 30% in the 2013 elections, and 41% in the European elections of 2014. The party had been the dominant force behind a series of coalition governments over five years, and had clearly worn out its welcome. Renzi (2014-2016) and his successor Paolo Gentiloni (2017-2018) had put an end to the harsh austerity of the previous technocrat governments, but it was not enough. The

---

4   In my July 2017 Italian-language book *The Revolt of the Voters*, I wrote: "The
      country in which the populists are most likely to make it into power is probably
      Italy..." Andrew Spannaus, *La rivolta degli elettori* (Sesto San Giovanni:
      Mimesis Edizioni, 2017), p. 9.

effects of the crisis were still widespread, and the EU budget rules were increasingly the key point of attack for the opposition parties.

The Five-Star Movement demanded stronger anti-corruption rules, cuts in the high salaries and pensions of public officials, and a basic income guarantee for the millions of people living in poverty. The latter would obviously require abandoning the notion of a balanced budget; and in fact the M5S heavily criticized EU economic policy, to the point of promising a referendum – the group's preferred decision-making mechanism, including internally – on whether or not Italy should stay in the Euro.

The "citizen's income" proposal raised the hopes of many in Italy's South, which is considerably poorer than the rest of the country, giving the M5S an electoral sweep across the *Mezzogiorno*. The proposal, although it was partially cut down to size when translated into law, is heavily criticized by many, particularly in the wealthier North. Yet the point was, and should still be, clear: if government policies have made people poorer, those people will be quick to vote for candidates who promise to go in a different direction.

The other big winner in the March 2018 elections was the League. Formerly the Northern League, the party was born and grew based on a separatist platform, calling for the wealthy and industrious North to split from Rome, which it claimed represented the lazy, inefficient South. This platform allowed the Northern League to elect mayors and regional governors across the North over the years, and play a role as a coalition member in the various governments led by Silvio Berlusconi between 1994 and 2011. The party gradually pulled back from its separatist aims, simply calling for greater autonomy; the anti-South rhetoric soon took a backseat to the focus on immigration, which emerged as a key issue starting in 2013, when the number of migrants from the Middle East and North Africa began to spike. The big change for the League came when Matteo Salvini took over the leadership of the party in December 2013. Salvini aimed high, seeking to expand the base beyond just the North, a geographical limitation that had kept the party between 5 and 10% at the national level for years.

The League's popular base had always been open to anti-globalization positions, being skeptical of not only immigration, but also the economic effects of the shift in power to financial interests, seen as representing an international oligarchy set on destroying tradition and economic well-being. Under Salvini, the party began to concentrate heavily on issues of this sort, taking aim in particular at the institutions seen as representing the interests of the elite, against those of 'regular people', starting with the structures of the European Union.

The overall shift was remarkable, although partially coherent in its own way. From a regional party calling for secession from the government in Rome, the League was now at the forefront of the "sovereignist" movement, demanding that decision-making power be returned to the national level, to protect against supranational imposition. The "coherence" comes from the fact that the League's targeting of international financial elites actually makes much more sense than its past prescriptions for dealing with the socio-economic decline seen in Northern Italy. Originally, the notion of a Republic of the North was presented in terms of a "Europe of Regions," i.e. more power locally, but without opposition to the consolidation of the European Union. In this way, the Northern League actually played into the process which it criticizes today.[5]

In the 2018 election campaign, the League became the most prominent Euroskeptic party. It ran economists who are strongly anti-Euro, such as Alberto Bagnai and Claudio Borghi, and ratcheted up the rhetoric against the EU, although remaining ambiguous on the promise of a referendum to leave the single currency. Salvini kept up his anti-immigration positions, but the League also adopted the clearest anti-globalization stance among the major political parties in Italy.

The result was spectacular. The League got 17% of the national vote in 2018, compared to only 4% in 2013. As the second-largest anti-establishment party, it ended up forming a coalition with the Five-Star Movement for the first populist government in Europe, with Salvini as Interior Minister and Deputy Prime Minister. He has used that position to clamp down on immigration, and to push the government to take a strong position against EU budget rules. Outside of Italy, Salvini is often seen as a dangerous right-wing populist, due to his harsh anti-immigration stance; inside the country, his popularity has ballooned, taking the League to over 30% in opinion polls, while support for the Five-Star Movement has begun to wane. Immigration is an important issue in Italy, the first point of entry for hundreds of thousands of migrants crossing the Mediterranean in recent years. But once again, it is political malpractice to deny the key role of the anti-globalization, anti-EU positions that have driven the League to such heights. The political elites of Europe do so at their own peril.

---

5   For a discussion of the League's history on Europe, see Andrew Spannaus, 'Catalonia and the Europe of Regions', *Consortium News*, October 11, 2017.

The stakes for Europe

The Italian government's first fight with the European Commission ended in a compromise: Italy will run a higher deficit than allowed under EU rules, but it also accepted what are called safeguard clauses which will trigger higher taxes and significant cuts in the future if economic conditions don't improve rapidly. The success in partially "taming" the Italian populists, bringing them to negotiate with the Commission rather than simply ignoring international pressure, certainly does not mean that opposition to the neoliberal aims of austerity, labor market flexibility, and financialization of the economy will go away. As noted, the poll numbers of the populist parties have grown in Italy, and once again street protests are increasing around Europe, as seen with the Yellow Vests movement in France, expressly seeking to defend the living standards of citizens who have suffered from the economic policies of the past decades.

Today it is even more important to deal with the fundamental mistakes made in recent years, lest the distrust of the institutions among the population become even deeper. It is counterproductive to write off the populists as incompetent, offensive rabble-rousers, against whom the only proper path is "resistance." The negative effects of globalization are real, and did not come about naturally, or inevitably. They are the product of specific political and economic decisions, that can be changed.

THE ORIGIN OF THE PROBLEM

The resistance of the political elites against populism consists of a defense of certain general principles, such as multiculturalism and economic openness. These are pillars of a model of shared cultural values and basic economic principles, seen as the inevitable framework of the future. There is nothing wrong with seeing progress in these terms; to the contrary, defending human rights and promoting economic growth are certainly positive goals. The problem emerges when these principles are used to justify policies that actually have other aims.

To understand the reversal of values carried out in recent decades, just think of the two concepts at the basis of Francis Fukuyama's thesis of the "End of History" in his celebrated essay of 1989: liberal democracy and the free market model. The West convinced itself that these two ideas represent the highpoint of human evolution, and that they would win out over other ideologies in the long term. However, this view of history and politics presents serious problems. Certainly not because I am against freedom and democracy, crucial values for Western civilization. Rather, these words have been exploited to pursue specific interests that have little to do with the general progress of the human race, or even only of the populations considered to be part of the Western liberal democratic model.

The examples of deception are in front of our eyes: in the name of democracy, we have promoted a series of wars over the past thirty years with devastating consequences for the Middle East. It could be argued that the original intention was positive, to export democracy to non-democratic countries, but it would still be very difficult to exculpate Western leaders – starting with the Bush and Obama administrations – for decisions on Iraq and Libya, and their (predictable) effects.

Consider also the unarmed interventions in numerous parts of the world that de facto only served to defend Western interests in a narrow sense, rather than promoting democracy. There is the case of Chile, where the United States contributed to the coup against President Salvador Allende in 1973, bringing to power the dictatorship of Augusto Pinochet. And more recently, the promotion of pro-Western formations throughout Eastern Europe in order to counter Russia has led to support for some groups that have little to do with democracy, such as the extreme right in Ukraine.

The issue of the free market, and whether this model actually promotes personal freedom, is even broader. It is widely claimed that liberal economics is the model that made the United States and many other Western countries great powers. The truth is different: the economic policies followed by the founding fathers from the 1700s forward had a strong component of protectionism and relied on the decisive role of the State. The "free market" was the model pursued by the British Empire, that aimed to keep the American colonies in a state of underdevelopment to ensure their domination from abroad.[1]

The basic outlook that allowed for great economic progress in the U.S. and Europe was still present just a few decades ago. On both sides of the Atlantic, the postwar period saw economic development by means of public policies that encouraged industrial growth and set rules to guarantee the proper functioning of markets. It was not an anti-market model, but a model which aimed to keep private interests from using the market to become more powerful than states. The efficacy of this approach has seen ups and downs in history, depending on how well it has been implemented and the extent of the opposition in various periods; but in recent times, the free market has often been used simply as a weapon to block public intervention, regardless of its economic effects for the majority of the population. The real goal has been the reduction of the sovereignty of nations, allowing private interests to decide economic policies without the difficulty of managing a colonial empire. In this context, the nation-state represents the true bulwark against oligarchies, offering governments the possibility to enact policies in favor of the general welfare.

---

1   For one treatment of the essential difference between the two economic systems of the time, see Henry C. Carey, *The Harmony of Interests, Agricultural, Manufacturing & Commercial* (New York: Augustus M. Kelley Publishers, 1967). More recently, on the "American System" of political economy, see Nancy B. Spannaus, *Hamilton versus Wall Street* (iUniverse, 2019).

The key point of the period of globalization that began in the 1990s is in fact the reduction of the role of nations and national governments. The increase of international trade, and the rapid technological leaps made (such as in the field of communications) have undoubtedly facilitated global integration and offered many positive opportunities for growth. The error was to allow greater trade and movement to become the justification for a policy that favored only the top, thanks to the weakness of states and the exponential increase of power exercised through finance. What was lost with the end of open colonialism, was in part regained with the assault on the nation-state through globalization.

The transformation began a long time ago, with the introduction of the concept of the post-industrial society in the 1970s. After a period of growth and progress in the initial decades following World War II, a major change in the structure of Western societies was theorized, and then gradually implemented. Assistance came from the first environmentalists, the oligarchical ones: the Club of Rome, the 1001 Club, and the World Wildlife Fund, the latter founded by Prince Philip of Britain and Prince Bernhard of the Netherlands. Dubious scientific theories, presented in books such as *The Population Bomb* by Paul Ehrlich (Sierra Club, 1968) and *The Limits to Growth* by Meadows and Forrester (Club of Rome, 1972), were used to argue against continued economic development.

One of the most visible effects was the perpetuation of poverty for decades in the so-called "Third World," countries that lived at subsistence level – or below – while "experts" in the West warned that the most serious danger was population growth, not the lack of basic infrastructure that could guarantee a decent life. Today there are many environmental problems facing the world, but it is sadly ironic that the policy of non-development caused harm principally to the poorest areas of the world. In Europe there are relatively strong laws against pollution, and although much remains to be done, institutional and social mechanisms exist to deal with environmental problems. In areas where poverty and war are common, the deterioration of the environment obviously takes a backseat to survival. In addition, the countries that have become important for outsourcing of Western industries often are in no condition to impose respect for basic environmental and labor regulations. The result is a process that has been poorly governed, driven by exploitation of human beings and natural resources, without considering its long-term harmful effects.

The other side of the coin is the financialization of the economy. From the 1970s on, there was a gradual process of growth of the importance of financial flows compared to activity in the real economy. This was not an inevitable change, but rather one facilitated by specific political decisions. The financial deregulation of the 1980s and 90s, which began in the United Kingdom and the United States, to then extend to other European countries, ultimately led to a world in which the fate of entire countries could be decided in a matter of days by groups of traders sitting in front of computer screens, or by those able to influence them. Globalization marked the defeat of the nation-state, allowing private financial interests to acquire a level of decision-making power that is difficult to define, but undoubtedly unprecedented.

Focusing on Europe, we see that in the 1990s, this process of elimination of national sovereignty took the concrete form of the European Union, which shifted the goal of strengthening the forms of international cooperation established during the course of the postwar period, to that of achieving a single supranational government for the entire continent. There are two questions to be asked: first, if this goal, which today is the subject of a deep political clash, is based on principles that are shared and beneficial for the citizens of the European countries involved; and second, if it is feasible in practical terms, that is, if a Europe without national sovereignty would truly reach its stated goals. I will deal with these questions in the next part of this book.

PART II

SIX CONTRADICTIONS FACING THE EUROPEAN UNION

WHAT GOOD IS EUROPE?

The European Union was born in 1957, with the Treaty of Rome, which established the European Economic Community (EEC). The EEC brought together the first group of Member States: France, West Germany, Italy, Belgium, the Netherlands, and Luxembourg. Along with the simultaneous creation of the European Atomic Energy Community, and the European Coal and Steel Community (1951), a period of cooperation began that would gradually lead to the European Union as we know it today. Over the years, various new countries joined, bringing the total number of Member States to 28 (which will drop to 27 if the United Kingdom leaves). Now there is an institutional structure that, thanks to numerous treaties and agreements, gives the Union a central role for all of the participants.

A large portion of national laws reflect EU legislation, or must at least be consistent with it. In 1988, Jacques Delors, then president of the European Commission, famously predicted that within 10 years, 80 per cent of national economic and social legislation would be decided at the European level. Estimates vary widely on what the real figure is now, depending on whether you count only the direct implementation of EU regulations or all laws and regulations that are linked to European-wide institutions,[1] but there is no doubt that nation-states have already delegated a broad component of their sovereignty to the EU, committing to follow common rules as they are adopted.

The process of integration is not complete, however. Supporters of greater centralization tout a vision of the "United States of Europe" as expressed by figures such as Altiero Spinelli and Jean Monnet in the 1950s. Yet the path that leads from Westphalia – the 1648 treaties symbolizing the affirmation of national sovereignty – to a cohesive

---

[1] See, for example, Clive Coleman, 'Reality Check: How much UK law comes from the EU', *BBC*, June 8, 2016.

European federation, has hit a rough patch. The legitimacy of the Union itself is being called into question by protest movements that oppose the role of supranational institutions and demand a return of power to the national level.

Each step towards greater integration has been met with some sort of skepticism, and thus has been duly 'sold' by the politicians in their respective countries. Today, for example, the defense of Europe against populism entails a series of references to shared goals and values – such as democracy, equality and respect for minorities – in the hope of avoiding the disintegration of the European project. Recently though, it has become much harder to convince people to support the process, for the reasons discussed in the introduction. The main problem is the identification of European policies with the weakening of the productive economy and the drop in living standards for the middle and lower classes, which have led to growing conflict both within Member States, and between them as well. At this point it becomes necessary to seriously reflect on the question: What justification is there for the European Union?

There are numerous answers proposed to this question today, ranging from the guarantee of peace and human rights, to economic necessity. No single response is offered by the supporters of the EU, but various arguments are given to convince citizens not to follow the appeals of the nationalists, presented with the conviction that the European Union truly is necessary to guarantee a positive future for all of its citizens. Below I will examine some of the main reasons cited by those who push for increasing integration.

1. *Peace*

The European Union has guaranteed "50 years of peace" between countries that went to war with each other for centuries, with tragic and unforgettable consequences. This is a claim that everyone has heard repeatedly in recent years. The implied corollary is that a return to national sovereignty would mean a return to war among European countries, and thus being against the EU is equivalent to being against peace.

The citizens of Europe have a history that is closely linked to past conflicts. Today the perception of common identity plays an important role, as people strive to see others as brothers and sisters, not enemies. Yet this recognition does not mean that the equivalence of "nations =

war" is proven. To claim that being against the European Union means taking us back to a period of open conflicts is the result of a series of a misunderstandings, whether intentional or not. The most important of these is the very definition of Europe. Today's EU is quite different from the European Communities that were begun in the 1950s. Cooperation between nations plays an essential role in creating close ties between peoples, and holds at bay the idea that others are fundamentally different and inevitably in competition with us. But the nature of cooperation has changed greatly over the past 60 years. In Europe, there is no longer a group of independent states that choose certain areas in which to pursue their common interests; rather, there exists a vast supranational structure that produces legislation in almost every field of economic and social life.

What is this "Europe" which is supposed to protect peace? The basic argument is that the Union produces permanent bonds among citizens from different nationalities, and that regardless of the problems that may arise, the alliance is necessary to never again return to the situation which produced millions of deaths in the World Wars. Yet to adopt this view, it is necessary to clearly define what these bonds are, since the argument for peace is used as a cudgel to force everyone to accept each additional step towards the common governance of European countries.

World War II ended in 1945. Thus, most of the "50 years of peace" now trumpeted by pro-integration politicians represent a period in which collaboration moved forward gradually, before shifting gears in the 1990s. The 1992 Maastricht Treaty, the key step towards today's form of union, went into effect almost 48 years *after* the end of hostilities. So it is a bit difficult to define the monetary union as a fundamental element of peace.

To go even further, we can point out that the common currency, the Euro, was created in 1999 as a unit of account, and became legal tender in 2002, almost 60 years after the end of World War II; hard to give the Euro any credit there. At the most we could speak of "15 years of peace," or at least of cohesion, since the advent of the single currency, but that would be quite a stretch, given the increasing divisions seen in Europe. And many of those divisions are linked precisely to the monetary policies claimed to be necessary to maintain financial stability as defined by the various EU rules, from the Maastricht Treaty to the subsequent Stability and Growth Pact, to the more recent accords such as the Fiscal Compact.

What stands out is the difference between the initial period of the European Union, from the fifties to the eighties, and the next phase, with the march towards full integration of economic and monetary policy. There is no need to be against European collaboration, or in favor of militaristic nationalism, to recognize the profound problems raised by the change in conception that took place starting in the nineties. What was previously an alliance between nation-states began to move towards a European superstate. That may be a legitimate goal for some, and it is clearly up to the citizens of Europe to decide if that is the direction they truly want to take; but the argument that European cooperation, as represented by today's supranational institutions, has been indispensable for peace is specious, and in some cases even dishonest.

2. *Democracy and Human Rights*

Another common argument in favor of the European Union is that it promotes democracy and represents a bulwark for human and civil rights in a world where those principles are constantly violated and ignored. This is an important statement of principle, based on numerous formal EU declarations and documents that commendably aim to guarantee the recognition and defense of human dignity. However, using this issue to defend greater integration leads to problems similar to those presented above regarding peace.

The Charter of Fundamental Rights of the European Union identifies a series of individual rights and freedoms, having the effect of law for the EU Member States. In postwar history though, the proclamation and protection of these rights does not derive from the EU, but depends on separate agreements such as the European Convention on Human Rights, adopted in 1950 by the Council of Europe, a body which is not part of the Union. In recent years, the decision was made to link EU rules to the Convention to create a more complete structure of laws, but that does not change the fact that the idea of Europe as a common space for freedom and rights has an origin independent of the EU institutions of Brussels and Frankfurt.

Incorporating pre-existing principles into EU law can be seen as a method to strengthen their acceptance, and provide a more binding framework to pressure countries into compliance. Yet here, too, things are complicated. Consider what has happened in recent years with immigration. The increase in the flow of migrants from Africa and the Middle East, as well as other areas of the world, is putting a heavy strain on the countries that initially receive them, such as Italy and Greece. As the Southern Europeans know, countries not on the front lines of the problem often shirk their responsibility to help under EU law, and do whatever they can to prevent migrants from heading further north, including closing internal European borders and building barriers.

So as the EU institutions affirm the rights of refugees upon their arrival at Europe's borders, some Member States feel they have been left to bear the burden by themselves, due to the power wielded by countries such as Germany, which successfully pushed for an agreement providing billions of Euros to Turkey to block the Balkan route that migrants took to reach Central and Northern Europe.

This does not mean that immigration problems are "Europe's fault," but it does show the weight of national interests when facing an emergency. The ideal of developing a common identity, in which the interests of all parts of the continent become the same, is attractive, but must face the fact that there are profound differences between the interests and problems that manifest themselves in different geographic areas, as well as the bureaucratic and social organization of the single Member States.

Then there is the question of popular will, because if Europe aims to promote human rights and democracy, it can certainly not ignore the expression of public opinion through democratic votes. If the elections in one Member State bring a political force to power that prefers a more restrictive approach towards immigration, for example, a problem arises. With the migrant crisis in recent years, some countries have been accused of violating European rules, leading to the activation of specific measures by the European Commission and disputes regarding respect for human rights. In the case of Hungary, the conflict with the EU sharpened and the government sought to bolster its position by demonstrating popular backing. Here a serious contradiction arises: common rules were agreed on at the EU level, without a popular vote, while referendums may be held to express a different opinion. Public support for such an opinion does not mean that general principles must be abandoned, but the conflict between democratically-elected politicians and supranational bureaucrats has become quite evident in recent years.

In addition, the principles of human rights are on quite a different level than, and even contradictory to, the monetary parameters of Maastricht, the Stability Pact, or the Fiscal Compact. So attempting to justify the overall structure of Europe by appealing to human rights is another of the misunderstandings in political discourse today. It is necessary to clearly distinguish between what Europe promotes and defends – and whether a supranational government is needed to do so – and the policies that regard other areas, which understandably benefit from much less support.

Moreover, it would be easy to demonstrate that EU economic policies actually violate certain rights, in particular social rights. The continuous demand to implement "structural reforms," that in practice often translate into harsh budget cuts, forces countries to reduce protections for their citizens. Has the EU defended the rights of the weakest members of society in Greece in recent years? In addition to demanding large cuts to pensions, allegedly justified by the need to combat waste, the "memorandum" agreements for Greece have led to a situation in which it is increasingly difficult to provide health care. Following the austerity imposed by Brussels and Frankfurt on Portugal, Italy, Ireland, Greece, and Spain – derisively called the "PIIGS" by some in Northern Europe – poverty increased sharply. So nobody should be surprised if the voters don't buy into the idea that the EU deserves support due to its promotion of human rights and democracy.

2.a. *The non-democratic construction of Europe*

One very sore point regarding the character of the European institutions is the lack of democracy in their construction. The goal of bringing together hundreds of millions of people, from countries with different histories and cultures going back thousands of years, is obviously difficult and requires an enormous public communications effort over time. What has been absent is popular participation in the decision to go forward.

The great phase shift represented by the 1992 adoption of the Maastricht Treaty was put to a popular referendum in only three countries: Ireland, France, and Denmark. The first two votes had positive outcomes, while the voters in Denmark initially rejected the Treaty, and then approved it in a second vote after the EU was forced to make concessions.[2] The other countries simply had the Treaty approved by their Parliaments, avoiding the risk of a popular rejection that would have been fatal for the project of the new Europe.

---

2   The Edinburgh Agreement of 1992 allowed Denmark to opt out of areas such as European citizenship, economic and monetary union, defense policy, justice, and home affairs.

The next big step towards the integration of European policies, despite not presented as such, was the Stability and Growth Pact of 1997, which strongly reduced the maneuvering room of single governments as they sought to meet the monetary parameters set by Maastricht. In his book *Non chiamatelo euro* ("Don't call it Euro") Italian journalist Angelo Polimeno presents the arguments of a famous jurist, Giuseppe Guarino, that demonstrate the illegitimacy of this change on a legal level.[3] The crucial point is that the Stability Pact is only a regulation, and thus does not have the legal force of the other European treaties. Elevating its precepts to the same level as the Maastricht Treaty, or even worse, going beyond the previous treaties with a simple regulation, would obviously be illegitimate, although this is exactly what happened. In addition to the serious economic effects of this decision, accompanied by constant disputes and divisions between European nations, the process has clearly not been democratic.

The attempt to adopt a European Constitution, on the other hand, was the subject of ample public debate. There was discussion of the Christian roots of Europe, of foreign policy and common defense, and of the best form for the supranational institutions. But when voting began, the plans to establish a European superstate were quickly wrecked. The first referendum was held in France in 2005, where the proposal for a constitution was soundly rejected, 55% to 45%. A few days later the Dutch went to the polls, to vote on the same question. The result was even stronger for the "no" side, which polled 62%.

At this point it became evident that the path towards the creation of a United States of Europe could not survive scrutiny from the people. From a democratic standpoint, two countries had already rejected the plan, and the idea of trying again seemed useless. A normal response would have been to acknowledge that the people were not ready for such a step, and thus to slow down the push for greater integration. Yet the leading institutional forces in Europe chose a different tack: given that the road towards a constitution was blocked, they simply turned onto another road – that of an intergovernmental treaty – starting the process that would lead to the enactment of the Lisbon Treaty in 2009.

Since a treaty does not have the same scope as a constitution, it was easier to justify approval only by national parliaments rather than consulting the people through a popular vote. So that's what happened, in almost all European countries. The next big step towards European

---

3   Angelo Polimeno, *Non chiamatelo euro* (Milan: Mondadori, 2015).

unity, that would entail further ceding of sovereignty to supranational structures, was approved without a real political debate, and with a popular referendum in only one country, Ireland.

What happened in Ireland with the referendum shows the preferred method of the European institutions to consolidate supranational power. First they set a goal, and then they find a way to reach it. If the majority of the powerful institutions are in favor, then the consent of the governed becomes only an annoying detail, as the path has already been decided.

Thus, when in 2008 the Irish rejected the Lisbon Treaty, the second attempt to strengthen supranational institutions at the expense of national sovereignty was also about to sink. But this time Brussels wasn't willing to give up: the idea was born to redo the referendum and use a series of carrots and sticks to convince the Irish to say "yes." Ireland obtained guarantees regarding constant representation on the European Commission, and leeway on issues such as taxation, military neutrality, and abortion. On the other hand, the "yes" side played up fears of disaster if Ireland were to be excluded from the EU.[4] The operation was successful, and in 2009 the Lisbon Treaty was saved. No other country dared put it to a vote of the people – Ireland is required to do so based on a decision of its Supreme Court – and thus the construction of Europe could go forward, but without broad-based democratic approval.[5]

Other important treaties were instituted in recent years, following the same method: the Fiscal Compact, which strengthens the budget parameters and establishes harsh sanctions for whoever does not respect them, and the European Stability Mechanism (ESM), an instrument to "save" states in financial difficulty, which offers loans in exchange for a sort of receivership by the European institutions, following the model of the International Monetary Fund's structural adjustment programs. These treaties do not rise to the level of constitutional law, but it is undeniable that they subtract additional portions of sovereignty from the Member States. The respective national parliaments approved them, but those who followed the legislative process know that there was no

---

4   For more detail, see Ece Özlem Atikcan, 'Asking the public twice: why do voters change their minds in second referendums on EU treaties?', *The London School of Economics and Political Science*, October 19, 2015.

5   This was actually the second time the two-referendum method had been used to ensure that Ireland would not block the approval of an EU Treaty. On June 7, 2001 the Irish rejected the Treaty of Nice. The Seville Declaration of June 21, 2001 addressed Ireland's reservations, on many of the same issues as those discussed in 2008.

real public debate. The parliaments acted in such a way as to avoid popular pressure in deference to the requests from "Europe."

This method of constructing the legal basis for the European Union raises serious questions: if the only way to move towards the creation of the United States of Europe is to circumvent the popular will, why is it necessary to pursue this goal? Shouldn't Europe be in favor of its own citizens? If the citizens are against a supranational government, what legitimacy could that government have?

The most common response to this complaint heard in recent years is one that expresses arrogance and circular reasoning: we need to construct the European Union precisely to meet the needs of the people, who will then realize why it's so important. So as we have seen, the model is to set a goal and then find the way to get there, democratically or not; a strange way to promote democratic values!

It could be objected that, if the people really were against the EU, then they would vote for anti-Europe parties, but this would also be a specious argument. For years, the political parties that have dared question the common currency were marginalized by the mass media and by existing political institutions. Recently though, in response to a socio-economic situation for which the EU is at least in part responsible, the parties that propose leaving the Euro or the European Union have grown, and their number has increased. Many of them use xenophobic and offensive language in doing so, and thus their support is lower than what could be expected with regard to only the EU question.[6] On the other hand, traditional political parties have worked hard to keep any expressions of anti-European positions outside of their ranks, thus forcing whomever is critical to remain on the margins of the system, and join groups that are seen as more extreme.

This model is now crumbling, not because the large political formations represented by the center-left and center-right parties have decided to revise their positions, but because their refusal to do so opened an enormous political space for protest parties. In this sense, the revolt of the voters is a clear and democratic response to the lack of democracy in the construction of the European Union.

---

6   This may seem counterintuitive, as some would suggest the fiery language actually draws more support, but the numbers show that the opposite is true. As discussed in the case of the various European elections of 2017-2018, support for parties critical of the European Union was generally much higher than support for only those who also identified with anti-immigration positions.

The irony is that when the Euroskeptics do make it into power, the pro-EU faction then says that past decisions cannot be modified. For example, in the Italian government's fight with the European Commission over deficit spending, a common refrain in the press was that Italy *chose* to submit to the criteria, so it's wrong to change now. The contradiction is all too obvious: the choice was made without any popular vote, while the current positions benefit from widespread support among the population.

3. *Economic Strength*

There are other arguments in favor of the European Union, like the importance of free circulation of persons and thus the creation of deeper cultural bonds. By now, the reader will have recognized the superficial nature of such claims, in line with what has been presented so far. To justify the removal of economic and military sovereignty because one can now easily pass through an airport without showing a passport, or with the wonderful experience of the Erasmus educational exchange program, is obviously a strained interpretation. Like these two examples, there are many practical advantages to European cooperation that have developed over the decades. Yet it is obvious that we must distinguish between useful agreements and practices, on the one hand, and the policies that are throwing the entire continent into crisis, on the other. To incessantly repeat that stopping the process of integration would mean losing all of the benefits produced by cooperation between nation-states shows once again the low level of respect for the intelligence of European citizens.

A more effective argument is that regarding the economy, i.e. the importance for European countries to join together in a world where the large actors, starting with the United States and China, are much bigger, and thus could end up crushing smaller countries that try to survive on their own on the international markets. The argument is that it is necessary to act as a single system, drawing on the strength of the European Common Economic Area, and equipping the supranational institutions with political powers allowing them to move as a single entity, and thus defend the interests of all Member States.

There are misunderstandings in this case as well. First of all, it is clear that the largest European countries already have a standing that allows them to survive on the international markets. Germany, France, and Italy are among the leading economic powers in the world. They became powerful thanks to their history and a very effective policy in the postwar period which allowed for rapid growth of industry, technology, and standards of living. To say that without the EU those countries would be lost, is a bit reductive. It also ignores the fact that the European common market and customs union predate Maastricht and the Euro, meaning that many of the benefits achieved from the 1950s until the early 2000s do not depend on the closer integration represented by the subsequent phases of the European Union.

Once again, this does not mean denying the importance and usefulness of many supranational instruments. Given the high level of integration among value chains in different countries, for example, facilitating trade and adopting common standards can certainly be beneficial. In addition, the European Union's structural funds and incentives make tangible contributions to economic activities from transport infrastructure to agriculture to small business development. The question is which of these measures benefit from being centralized at the supranational level, and which can be just as effectively – or even more effectively – implemented through legislative power at the national level, or regulated by bilateral or multilateral treaties. There is no question but that most European countries did an excellent job growing their economies for years while they made sovereign decisions.

The situation is certainly different today, but many of the problems from which productive economies have suffered in recent years are the result of a series of choices made by the transatlantic political and financial establishment. The neoliberal policies of globalization, with the encouragement of delocalization of production and the creation of an incredibly favorable climate for financial speculation, were gradually assimilated by national governments, often encouraged precisely by the European Union. It is the EU that prohibits state intervention, it is the EU that requests liberalization and privatization, and it is the EU – through the European Central Bank – that has supplied massive amounts of liquidity to the financial sector, while at the same time imposing austerity on the population.

The European institutions are populated by politicians and bureaucrats, who come from the various Member States, so the EU is not simply an abstract oligarchy. While on the one hand the most powerful states in the alliance, such as Germany and France, have outsized power in determining the direction of policy, on the other, the EU rules have taken on a life of their own, becoming a dogma strenuously defended by the supranational bureaucracy. Indeed, it is clear that the most effective tool for imposing the pro-austerity, pro-speculation policies has been the EU itself. Each time a Member State considers changing course, the pressure from Europe increases, and often includes the threat of legal action. The fear that someone could break with what we could call the "Brussels Consensus," i.e. the monetarist and neoliberal policies imposed by the Troika, leads the European institutions and their supporters to do everything they can to guarantee their own supremacy, to the point of organizing changes of governments, as seen in Greece and Italy just a few years ago.[7]

It is certainly true that a single nation of almost 500 million people would count more on the international scene than a series of smaller nations. The fundamental problem is that European economic policies, from the Maastricht Treaty forward, have supported and promoted the process of industrial decline that has led to the current difficulties. The notion of joining together in the name of a failed policy is reckless to say the least. A more reasonable path would be to redefine Europe's goals based on new assumptions, more attuned to the well-being of the population. Perhaps in certain fields it really does make sense to join together, but it is impossible to assess such a need when the structure of European institutions is based on an economic architecture whose foundations are crumbling right at this time.

Trade deals under fire

The negotiations on trade deals are a good example of the dilemma. Until 2016, the EU institutions affirmed the need for a new agreement with the United States, the "Transatlantic Trade and Investment Partnership," or TTIP. Like other large international agreements of its kind, the main goal was to further liberalize trade, eliminating tariff and non-tariff barriers to economic exchange. What many ultimately understood, however, is that the current model of free trade mainly facilitates the search for low costs, and thus benefits multinational corporations, while creating more than a few problems for economies with a broad base of small and medium-sized enterprises, where the quality of processes and human resources are the most important factors. Taking additional steps towards a market that is freer, but in which that freedom mostly benefits the largest players, is not a winning

---

7   See footnotes 10 and 11 on page 24.

model for many countries, and certainly not for those in Europe that rely more on quality than quantity.

There are undoubtedly specific sectors in which European industries would gain an advantage from new free trade deals, given the many highly-productive manufacturing companies that aim to further increase their exports; but the credibility of the theorem that "liberalization = economic growth" is falling rapidly. Competition must lead upwards, which also means protecting the weakest members of society. Major trade deals perpetuate a model which has already caused a lot of damage, and the Europeans are now aware of this.

The charge that large trade deals bring negative side effects for certain sectors of the economy is nothing new. Indeed, at the highest level of Western institutions, the push for new pacts was not justified principally by their economic effects, but by their strategic import. In February 2015, I interviewed Jamie Shea, Deputy Assistant Secretary General for Emerging Security Challenges at NATO in Brussels. In discussing the TTIP and its companion deal, the Trans-Pacific Partnership, the 12-country accord proposed by the United States with other countries along the Pacific Rim, Shea made it clear that the most important goal was to counter the emerging "anti-Western narrative" coming from powers such as Russia, China, and Brazil. He said that in order to combat the authoritarian capitalist powers, it was necessary to bind liberal democracies together, and make sure that "Western liberal rules are going to dominate the 21st Century."

In conclusion, Shea told me:

> Let's face it, if you're going to do this, you can have all the defensive arrangements that you like, but to have a Trans-Pacific Partnership and a Trans-Atlantic Partnership at the same time, as complementary elements in the two most important strategic areas of the world, the Pacific and Europe – Europe may not be the world's most dynamic economy at the moment, but it certainly is one of the most strategic areas of the world – this is to my mind the equivalent of the Marshall Plan. [..] That's why this is much more important than arguing about chlorinated chickens.

The "chlorinated chickens" quip referred to worries in Europe about having to accept poultry from the U.S. that is treated with certain chemicals not allowed in the EU. On a host of agricultural and health issues, Europeans have more restrictive rules, and they worry that a common market with America would be a blow to the quality of their products. What Shea's remark showed is that for some, the effects of the trade deals on consumers or businesses is only a secondary consideration; the pacts were more properly seen as strategic instruments whose aim was to isolate China and Russia.

It's not a great discovery to find that political institutions don't always pursue the true interests of the population, especially when strategic goals are involved. The push to implement neoliberal economic policies, regardless of their effects on product quality or labor conditions, has been quite common in recent decades. Yet the case of the large trade deals once again shows the danger of assuming that by joining together, European countries will necessarily achieve a better outcome. Rather, the use of a supranational institution can make it harder for democratic opposition to check decisions made for other reasons.

4. *United States vs. Europe?*

Now I want to address the question of the attitude of the United States towards the European Union. We often hear that the United States is scared of the growth of a united Europe, which could compete with America's economic dominance. A common reaction to any criticism of the goal of European integration expressed by an American is that there's obviously a bias, i.e. the desire to block the growth of a stronger union and thus favor American interests.

It is fairly easy to demonstrate the weakness of this argument. To start with, all that is required is an honest look at the situation of Europe today. As has been amply explained above, the principal cause of the economic difficulties of European countries today is represented precisely by the dogmatic, and almost religious, adherence to the policies proposed by the Union itself. Austerity, the restriction of public investment and regulation of the economy, and a monetary policy that favors the domination of private financial interests, are European countries' greatest enemies. The United States certainly has nothing to fear from a situation in which some of the most productive and developed countries in the world submit to a policy dictated by the current political and financial elites. Actually, that is exactly how to guarantee a weak Europe in the future.

It is true that some sectors of the U.S. institutions could be suspicious of Europe as a united entity if it truly were able to prevail in competition with the United States. But this worry has not translated into hindering the construction of the European Union. The opposite is true. The U.S. establishment has repeatedly encouraged close ties between the institutions on both sides of the Atlantic. This is why, starting with deregulation in the 1980s, through the financial explosion of the 1990s and the market crashes of the 2000s, Europe and the United States have generally shared the same fate. There are differences between the economies in the Western world, in terms of composition, flexibility, and degree of liberalization. The overall direction, though, is very similar, as also demonstrated by the political reaction among the population in the entire transatlantic area.

A practical example of the close ties between the United States and Europe is found in the response to the crash of 2008, followed shortly afterwards by the crisis of the Euro. Between 2009 and 2011, the U.S. Federal Reserve provided massive amounts of liquidity to the ECB to help it stabilize the financial markets. This was done through the mechanism of swaps between the central banks, to avoid the impression of direct aid to European banks from the U.S. By making tens of billions of dollars available, the United States played a key role in *saving* the Euro!

The obvious explanation for this intervention is that there are immediate common interests. The failure of European banks would have had harsh consequences for U.S. financial institutions, given the level of international integration. This is one of the reasons that the elites on both sides of the Atlantic are so closely linked, and why the goal of stability is always primary. So for the most part, American institutions saw the EU as important for guaranteeing the continuity of shared policies at the highest level.

With the arrival of the Trump Administration, things have changed, at least in part. The current U.S. President is skeptical of supranational institutions, preferring to work at the bilateral level. Political relations in Europe are already changing, due to Brexit and the growth of internal pressure for a change in EU institutions. However, despite the orientation of President Trump, change is more likely to be limited than profound on this point. There are opportunities for individual European countries to exploit the situation offered by the new orientation of the current administration, but a complete break between Washington and Brussels is unlikely.

The real challenge is not between the United States and Europe; it is between the elites that have governed our world over the last 40 years, pursuing the interests of the better-off portions of society, and those who aim to promote the interests of the entire population. It is between those who are unable to see the need for a change of course, and those who recognize that for the entire Western world, the current policies are no longer sustainable, and could lead to upheaval on an even greater scale than seen in the last few years.

5. *Common Defense*

The idea of developing a common defense capacity has existed from the beginning of the process of European cooperation in the 1950s. Today even those who are skeptical of greater economic integration often claim that an area in which closer ties makes sense is that of military equipment and deployments. The convenience for countries less used to international interventions, or those that are convinced that such deployments must always take place in the context of supranational bodies such as the United Nations, is undeniable. Many countries contribute to numerous missions under the aegis of the UN and NATO, that would be impossible for them to organize individually.

Yet there are important issues to be clarified in this field as well. First of all, the ultimate goal must be defined. The elephant in the room is the EU's close relationship with NATO. Given that almost all European countries are members of the Atlantic Alliance, the idea of creating an independent decision-making structure could indeed be seen as a threat to the predominant role of the United States. This does not mean that a choice to go in a new direction would be illegitimate. It would be a big step though, that would certainly require a serious discussion of Europe's strategic vision for the future. The Lisbon Treaty recognizes this ambiguity, providing the reassurance that NATO "remains the foundation of [member states'] collective defense and the forum for its implementation."[8] Yet it is no secret that many see European common defense as a way of creating a distinction between the continent's interests and those of the United States; again, legitimate, but not a step to be taken without clearly defining the desired path.

Another problem that arises regards the mechanism for making decisions. Even in the event of a simply "practical" structure for capacity

---

8   Treaty of Lisbon amending the Treaty on European Union and the Treaty establishing the European Community, Article 42.

sharing, it would be necessary to define the areas of competence. If integrated forces were to be created with troops and equipment from multiple countries, who would decide how to deploy them? A 27-member Council, with each country having veto power? That is what the Lisbon Treaty currently prescribes, for "decisions relating to common security and defense policy."

Given the considerable differences among EU countries as regards foreign policy, the risk is that the largest countries, those who have greater military capacity, would attempt to impose their decisions on the others. One example suffices to understand the nature of the problem: that of the 2011 war in Libya, in which the intent – and interests – of Italy and France were decidedly different.[9] The result of this type of situation would be temporary paralysis, and then the inevitable decision of the more interventionist countries to act on their own, through some other mechanism, without waiting for the assent of the other member states.

The Lisbon Treaty provides for precisely such a mechanism: "enhanced cooperation." While unanimous consent is necessary to decide on the general policy, the execution of a mission can be entrusted "to a group of Member States in order to protect the Union's values and serve its interests."[10] In addition, "permanent structured cooperation" is to be established among "Member States whose military capabilities fulfill higher criteria and which have made more binding commitments to one another in this area with a view to the most demanding missions." And in this context, the "decisions and recommendations" are made "by the participating Member States only".[11]

It is not hard to see how a few large countries could *de facto* dominate common defense policy. For some, that may seem a reasonable trade-off, to provide the EU with a common foreign and security policy. Yet once again the risk is to put the cart before the horse: to say that common defense is needed seems to respond to certain practical needs, but it does not resolve the differences in the views and interests between different countries, which are not merely perceived, but based on real historical, geographic, and political factors. Attempting to overcome them through a strained attempt at a stronger form of union could produce the same

---

9   See Andrew Spannaus, 'For Italy, Trump Represents a 'Populist' Opportunity', *Consortium News*, August 16, 2018.

10   Treaty of Lisbon…, Article 42.

11   *Ibid*. Article 42, Article 46.

effects already seen in the economic sphere, with the same limits on democracy as well.

5.a *Europe's strategic position*

The more general issue is the strategic position of Europe, and thus its relationships with the areas to its East and South. The expansion of NATO to include the countries of Eastern and Southeastern Europe was driven more by foreign policy considerations than by a sense of common identity; the goal was – and is – to expand the Western alliance to the detriment of Russia, which, in the 1990s in particular, found itself in a position of weakness and transition. Entry into the European Union today is seen as a step towards inclusion in NATO, such as in the case of Ukraine. The problem is that here as well, the policy has been imposed from the top down, i.e. a strategic goal has driven a process for which other justifications have been provided to the public.

The West is at a geopolitical fork in the road: continue to focus on conflict with Russia, or return NATO to a defensive posture, without seeking further expansion. This is the logical conclusion of the approach adopted by Donald Trump, who would like better relations with Russia, and to withdraw troops from the conflict areas in the Greater Middle East.

The question of NATO's position is obviously crucial for the foreign policy orientation of European countries, and the EU as a whole. Two years into his term, President Trump's desire to shift NATO away from an adversarial stance towards Russia appears to be failing; the July 2018 summit in Helsinki, for example, was overshadowed by the engineered hysteria over Russiagate, forcing Trump to step back from his plans to announce steps forward in areas such as industrial cooperation and cybersecurity, not to mention a second summit with Vladimir Putin a few months later.

It thus appears unlikely that the current U.S. Administration will succeed in making a lasting policy shift. Yet for many large European countries, a change of this type would be welcome, as they seek to maintain mutually beneficial economic relations with Russia, and also to avoid an increase in tensions that would once again put Europe in the position of a junior partner of the United States, stuck between two superpowers fighting for influence over their territories and populations.

On the other hand, there are some members of the EU that would not welcome rapprochement with Russia at all. Poland, or the Baltic states of Lithuania, Latvia, and Estonia – all former victims of Soviet imperialism – are unlikely to acquiesce to the goals of EU members such as Germany, France, and Italy. Once again, we see that while the idea of forming a common defense for Europe may be attractive in theory, contradictions would arise immediately regarding the most important strategic decisions facing the Western world.

6. *Geopolitics*

The last justification for the construction of a strong EU that we will discuss is that of the balance of power within Europe itself, that is, the geopolitical strategy used to guarantee international equilibrium over the past 70 years.

Geopolitics is a concept developed by the British geographer Halford Mackinder at the start of the last century, which indicates the influence of geographic factors on political decisions. In 1904, Mackinder wrote that the key to global domination was the control of the "heartland", i.e. of the Eurasian continent. It was precisely in that period that the British Empire identified its main objective for the subsequent decades: limit the growth of Germany, and above all block the possibility of a continental alliance between Germany, France, and Russia, that could mark the end of the golden age of an empire on which "the sun never sets."

The events that led to World War I have a common theme, the risk that Germany could become so strong as to dominate Europe and also expand its power towards the Middle East. This area began to become extremely important when it was recognized that oil would play a crucial role in the economic and military strategies of the years to come. The Germans aimed to create a direct connection with Mesopotamia, for example through the Berlin-Baghdad railroad, that would allow not only access to new energy resources, but also the possibility of surpassing the influence of its principal competitors, France and Great Britain.

The contest for supremacy in Europe, or better, to avoid German supremacy, has dominated European history for more than a century. The end of the Great War led to the imposition of harsh conditions on Germany that contributed to the rise of the Nazis, and thus the outbreak of World War II, with millions of deaths and unprecedented destruction of economic and social resources. After the war, a period of growth and well-being began, which created the world as we know it today.

The greater cohesion between European countries from 1945 on is due principally to a strategic driver: the need to counter the advance of the Soviet Union, and thus the importance for the United States, through NATO, to defend Europe as a whole. The nations of Western Europe came together in a military alliance to defend their freedom, and they did so under the protective umbrella of the most powerful country in the world. As internal European conflicts moved to the back burner, numerous possibilities for practical integration arose. There was strategic value to closer ties, through the establishment of the European Communities, which were not opposed, but rather encouraged, by the United States. Marshall Plan funds, for example, were conditional upon collaboration between European countries.

With the end of the Cold War, the situation changed, and worries again arose regarding the outsized power of Germany. Reunification brought fears of a German resurgence and a return to the military disasters of the start of the century. The British, in particular, led a public campaign to label Germany as the "Fourth Reich," thus raising the specter of the return of Nazism, and aimed to block Germany's rise before it could begin. This is when the Euro was born.

The new phase of the European Union, its transformation from an alliance between sovereign states to a project for the creation of a supranational superstate, is rooted in this desire to put Germany in a straitjacket. The main tool in this plan, led by François Mitterrand's France and Margaret Thatcher's United Kingdom, with the help of U.S. President George H.W. Bush, was the single currency. The control of currency is the crucial mechanism to remove a nation's sovereignty, and thus the construction of a common monetary policy was a guarantee of external control able to limit German power.

This goal was not a secret; it was and is well-known among the European governing class. From a historical and political standpoint, the various arguments on the importance of Europe discussed above are all secondary with respect to this one: the perceived need to squeeze Germany in a geopolitical embrace, and thus block the path towards renewed German supremacy.

Years later, Helmut Kohl himself wrote in his memoirs of the dilemma he faced when Mitterrand and Thatcher imposed the Euro on Germany. The Chancellor wrote that, in order to obtain France and Britain's support for reunification, he was forced to accept the single currency. According to Kohl, this was actually a decision that went against his country's interests, although today it is not hard to see that in some areas, Germany has actually benefitted significantly from the structure of the common market.

The economic paradigm shift

The geopolitical objective behind the creation of Europe brought with it some side effects that would contribute significantly to the socio-economic crisis in Europe today. The need to limit Germany's sovereignty led by extension to the limitation of the sovereignty of other large European countries as well. A supranational structure was established that made it possible for Western elites – the ruling class that represents powerful political and financial interests – to pursue their own interests and avoid unwelcome initiatives by national leaders. By embracing the EU, decision-making authority would be removed from individual countries and concentrated in certain supranational bodies, making it easier for unelected forces to exert their influence.

This reduction of national sovereignty represented a great opportunity for oligarchical interests, as it coincided with the start of a phase of transformation of Western economies. After the introduction of the notion of the post-industrial society starting in the 1970s and the first round of significant deregulation in the 1980s, at the beginning of the 1990s the power of finance was on the rise. The expansion of the use of financial derivatives fed a parasitic speculative bubble whose value was much greater than the GDP of the entire world – although those values were essentially fictitious and largely divorced from sustainable wealth. In the 1990s, this financial explosion was facilitated by a series of further regulatory changes, that aimed at opening up various sectors of the productive economy to financial capital, and thus provide new underlying assets on which to construct speculative schemes.

These changes, which in Europe marked the abandonment of the "social market economy" pursued with great success in the postwar period, would certainly have encountered greater resistance if left to the discretion of national governments, without outside constraints. The fault, of course, lies with the national politicians who allowed this to happen, but it is undeniable that the neoliberal model which guided the European institutions was the driver of the transformation.

Germany was famous for its "Rhine model" of capitalism. This was certainly not the guiding principle of the policies adopted for the integration of East Germany. Rather, the method followed was "shock therapy," the theory developed by schools in Britain and the United States, led by Professor Jeffrey Sachs of Harvard University. According to the definition provided by the International Monetary Fund, this was a combination of liberalizations, privatizations, and financial stabilization, implemented for example in many countries of the former Soviet bloc. The shock led to considerable economic suffering and imbalances, such as the emergence of the infamous "oligarchs." More generally, Germany came closer to the orientation of the "Washington Consensus," through financial operations and austerity policies, despite maintaining significant industrial strength.

In Italy, an entire political class was wiped out by the scandals of *"Tangentopoli"* (Bribe City), bringing to power a group of people who would contribute to re-writing the rules of the country's economy, ranging from Carlo Azeglio Ciampi and Giuliano Amato, to Romano Prodi and Mario Draghi (Draghi is now the President of the European Central Bank). The new pro-EU and pro-finance governments – interrupted from time to time by Prime Ministers who were less technocratic and more political, and thus less zealous in following the diktats of the new financial powers – were essential for the construction of European policy. Despite all of their defects, the politicians of the so-called "First Republic" in Italy, the period from the close of World War II to the transformation of 1992-93, had definitely shown more resistance to the elimination of their decision-making power.

The main motivation behind the creation of the new European Union – the EU born with the Maastricht Treaty in 1992 and based on monetary criteria, austerity, and an economic model consistent with financial globalization – was the limitation of the national sovereignty of the Member States. The initial target was Germany, but the model worked quite well in the service of a broader design, that of continuing the economic policies preferred by the Western elites from the 1970s on. Those are the policies that led to the reduction of productive industry, the increase of unstable working conditions and growing imbalances between the minority of society, that benefits from the world of high-level financial services, and the majority, which finds it increasingly difficult to maintain a decent standard of living. These are the policies that provoked the revolt of the voters across the transatlantic world, which if they are not changed, could destroy not only the model of the European Union of the past twenty-five years, but also those forms of more limited, but positive, cooperation that have existed for well over fifty years.

CONCLUSION:
THE FUTURE OF EUROPE

It is often said that the solution is "more Europe." Faced with any political, economic or strategic difficulty, EU believers assure us that if there were only full political integration, a recognition of the continent's common interests, then any problems could be dealt with better. There is no doubt that in most cases this conviction is expressed in good faith. There are many politicians, and a significant part of the population – younger people, in greater percentages – who see Europe positively and envisage supranational institutions that can truly respond to people's needs. Yet the rallying cry of "more Europe" raises many doubts, because it reflects complete faith in the form of the EU, rather than the substance.

Considering what we have presented above, it is clear that "Europe" as a common entity is not based on a clear and shared vision. The historical motivation for a European superstate came principally from geopolitical factors; the attempt to convince everyone to become pro-EU based on a guarantee of peace, the defense of human rights, or economic well-being, suffers from numerous contradictions.

The main problem is the tendency to put the cart before the horse. Claiming that the only way to solve Europe's problems is with more integration, suggests that in order to deal with the substance, there first has to be a new form. The justification for this is not clear. What prevents today's European institutions from addressing the mistakes made from the nineties on? There has been a limited debate on the failure of austerity, but recent events show that the monetary orthodoxy lives on. The budget parameters and "free market" rules limiting state intervention are alive and well, based on their codification in European treaties and regulations. To say that more Europe is needed without revising instruments such as the Fiscal Compact that sets mandatory budget balancing rules which many Member States – or at least their citizens – find repugnant, makes a mockery of the claims to be pursuing the best interests of the European population.

The construction of a 'United States of Europe' would require more or less uniform legislation across the continent. Currently, there are significant differences among countries, which give rise to numerous contradictions. The fact is, that these differences reflect the history and characteristics of each country. They cannot be changed by decree. The only possibility, which seems to be the goal of the authors of the European Monetary Union, is to force everyone to adopt a common model. That immediately poses the question: which model? That of widespread entrepreneurship, with many small and medium-sized enterprises, such as in Italy and Germany? Or a different model, tailored more to large multinational corporations and global financial markets?

These are questions regarding substance, and cannot be solved by putting the cart of supranational institutions out in front. First, it is necessary to decide what model to pursue, and given the results obtained by the Troika over the years, and the public protests that have exploded recently, it would be reckless and arrogant to presume that the model currently enshrined in the European treaties from Maastricht on, is the right one.

At the level of realpolitik, the justification for attempting to force European countries to accept a new form of European Union without much debate is quite clear. The system of central banks, and the political and financial interests they cater to, certainly does not want to see a sudden change of course. The election of Donald Trump in the United States, and the growth of populist movements across Europe, with a renewed focus on protectionism to favor domestic production, are threats to the free market model of the past decades. Trump's movement in this direction has been only partial, as he tends to use tariffs as a weapon to obtain concessions from other countries and change the trade agreements of the past, while simultaneously supporting certain aspects of deregulation. To date, the result has been a limited shift in the overall economic situation; much remains to be done to break the substantial continuity of neoliberal policies in the U.S.

The EU institutions, however, have been quick to proclaim their opposition to protectionism in any form, and to move rapidly to counter actions that could portend a return to state intervention on a significant scale. The reason is more practical than theoretical: if you allow one country to break the rules, the floodgates could open to a widescale repudiation of the free market policies of the past 25 years. This is why the Troika maintained such a hard line with Greece during the 2015 negotiations over the "memorandum" with the EU and the repayment of the country's foreign debt. And also why the European Commission fought so hard to block the Italian government from deviating from the march towards a balanced budget.[1] If one country can openly challenge the rules, what will stop others from doing the same? This is the same concern that led to the creation of the Euro: the goal is to guarantee common policies, easily managed from the top down, without the danger that national governments could exercise their sovereignty in conflict with the desires of Brussels and Frankfurt, as well as of London and New York.

In the long term, this is a lost cause. Not due to personal opinions or insidious conspiracies against the European Union; simply, the failure of the pro-finance, anti-real economy model can no longer be ignored. However much the supranational institutions aim to avoid the criticism from the voters and guarantee their own control in the interest of a model that principally favors the wealthier segments of society, reality will ultimately assert itself. There must be a return to representative government, to the instruments that were used to construct the well-being of the Western world in the decades after World War II, and even earlier. There must be a return to the role of the State, the political vehicle best suited to make those changes, in opposition to rule by private interests that by definition, do not pursue the common good. This does not mean it is necessary to exclude supranational cooperation through collective bodies. The European Union could, in theory, reform and become more responsive to the needs of the people, but until that happens, and people are represented by democratically-elected institutions that pursue their best interests, increasing the power of supranational organizations means doing the bidding of those whose goals do not favor the general welfare.

A return to health

Europe aims to become stronger on the global chessboard. Between the U.S., Russia, and China, European countries risk being caught in the middle of more powerful strategic actors, at the mercy of both conflicts and agreements between others. Europe has an interest in maintaining a privileged relationship with the United States, but also in continuing economic relations with Russia and developing those with Asia. The

---

1   See Andrew Spannaus, 'The Euro-Establishment's Fear of Populism', *Consortium News*, December 21, 2018.

opportunities are too great to ignore, in particular for those economies that can provide the capital goods and essential know-how for the growth of new partners in other areas of the world.

The question is, how to become stronger. Here again, we should look at the example of the United States. The Obama Administration adopted a policy to protect the West's interests with respect to the rise of China. Obama launched the "Pivot to Asia," a two-pronged strategy consisting of a further increase of America's military presence in the area, and a new trade agreement that was to exclude China, the Trans-Pacific Partnership (TPP). The TPP succumbed to public pressure during the 2016 election campaign, however. Donald Trump constantly attacked the deal, identifying it with the continuation of the arrangements that had facilitated the loss of productive jobs to low-labor countries. Bernie Sanders also firmly opposed the pact, and as a consequence even Hillary Clinton promised to block the treaty if she were elected, although there were legitimate doubts as to her sincerity.

One of President Trump's first acts in office was to withdraw from the TPP. The majority of American institutions were quite unhappy, as they had bought into the notion that the deal would "make sure that the United States – and not countries like China – is the one writing this century's rules for the world's economy",[2] a concept often repeated by Obama. Above all, the trade pact was seen as a means to strengthen alliances with friendly countries against the unwelcome growth of other powers, as stated bluntly by Jamie Shea in the quote cited in section 3. – Economic Strength, above. The 2016 elections, however, showed that due to the real problems created by the trade policies of the last few decades, such a geopolitical motivation is not enough, at least for the voters. The problem was that in this case, strengthening the position of the United States and its allies required a trade pact that would continue to weaken the middle class.

So what path should the West follow? If not through economic alliances such as the TTIP and the TPP, how can Western nations face the global challenges of the twenty-first century? The question affects Europe in particular, which finds itself in the middle of a global power struggle. The response, once again, does not allow for shortcuts, but is to be found in the substance of economic policy. If European countries wish to effectively compete on international markets, if they want to

---

2   'President Obama: "Writing the Rules for 21st Century Trade"', *The White House*, February 15, 2018.

play the role of key partner for the development of emerging economies, they must rely on their points of strength. This means abandoning faith in the "magic of the market," or to be more precise, in management based on a strictly financial mentality, rather than on the logic of production. Services are very important, and represent an advantage for Western economies. Yet it would be suicidal to think that services should now be dominant, and thereby give up the leading role achieved in technology and cutting-edge processes sustained by a workforce with great experience and skills.

Innovation and quality are the keys to growth. To achieve them political guidance is required; and political guidance requires effective governments. A strategy is needed to manage the digital evolution of production, in order to enhance manufacturing skills, not abandon them. This means development that invests in efficiency in order to raise the quality of economic activities, rather than exploit changes for short-term gain, damaging both the social fabric and the natural environment. A necessary precondition is public investment in hard and soft infrastructure, and a fiscal policy that encourages productive activity in the private economy.

Large processes can and must be governed. Markets must be regulated. Government incentives must be provided. The alternative is that other forces will decide the future of Europe, from outside interests and events, to a short-sighted elite that continues to pursue its own goals over those of the many. From the 1970s on, these forces have led to a gradual hollowing out of the middle class, a process that accelerated rapidly starting in the 1990s. The result has been an explosion of the protest against the organizations and people who facilitated and defended these changes. Now is the time to face the substance of these problems and avert a situation in which the same policies are continued through a mere change in form.

The success of new parties and outsider candidates who have challenged the political class that managed the post-industrial transformation of the past 40 years, can be seen as a threat to be countered, or an opportunity to shift gears. The entire Western world is grappling with a revolt that, for now, is expressed through the electoral process; the right response is to break with past mistakes, and return to the promotion of the common good and the general welfare.

EPILOGUE:
RETURN TO WESTPHALIA

The broad issues behind the revolt of the voters that has put populists in government in the United States and Italy, and led to the growth of outsider parties across Europe as a whole, have a common denominator: sovereignty. There is strong opposition to economic and financial globalization which has favored outsourcing of labor and allowed speculative finance to acquire enormous power over the policies of States. This is all based on the elimination of borders, especially in economic terms: by now, large corporations and capital operate unhindered around the world, a factor which heavily conditions the decisions of governments, that must deal with the new reality of the "international markets," often more powerful than national laws.

The change has been decisive in foreign policy as well. With the promotion of a system of internationally shared principles, the respect for national sovereignty has faded into the background. Military interventions aimed at "regime change," or based on the notions of "humanitarian intervention" and the "right to protect" – two sides of the same coin – affirm the supremacy of democratic values as defined by the Western establishment, over national prerogatives.

This is a fundamental change: the abandonment of the principles of the Peace of Westphalia, the accord that put an end to the Thirty Years War in 1648, and laid the basis of international law for hundreds of years to come. The concept of Westphalia was simple: "States are responsible for their own territory and citizens and that other states shouldn't interfere with either."[1] The first article of the treaty signed in Münster, Germany, even spoke of the requirement for the parties to "endeavor to procure the benefit, honor and advantage of the other." Thus, nations are called on to respect the rights of others and work towards their

---

1   Stephen M. Walt, 'Could there be a Peace of Trumphalia?', *Foreign Policy*, Jan. 14, 2016.

realization, rather than seek to extend their imperial dominion. This was the basic principle of relations between Western states for three centuries, although violations were frequent, for example when dealing with other areas of the world, as demonstrated by colonial policies.

The failure of the Western elites has been strictly linked to the abandonment of the concept of sovereignty. A certain view of the world, to be implemented with instruments that at times are democratic, and at times are not, facilitated the policies that have provoked discontent among large segments of the population, that in turn see these "values" of globalization as a threat not only to their own well-being, but even more so, to their identity.

Today, the idea of a return to "nationalism" is considered dangerous, negative by definition, being associated with the wars of the past. A more serious examination of the issue, however, shows that the concept of national sovereignty could be particularly important precisely to combat the perpetuation of the Western world's most serious errors over the past four decades: a foreign policy based on unjustified and counterproductive military interventions, and economic policies that are now backfiring against those who benefitted from them, as they foolishly thought they could ignore the consequences on the majority of the population.

Blaming the form of the nation-state for the wars of the past is another transparent deception. Indeed, what is the alternative? The model of the 'United States of Europe' is still based on that of sovereignty, simply at a higher level than that of single European countries. The name itself proves this goal, as an imitation of the American form of federalism. The reality is that there are only two alternatives to the existence of nation-states: empires, or supranational government. It is not uncommon to hear of the stability produced by empires in past millennia. The other side of the coin was economic and social stagnation with poor living conditions not only for the subjugated periphery, but also within the empires themselves, at least for most of the population. Times were different, and we can certainly debate which empires did better or worse, but it is no coincidence that the growth of population and the explosion of culture and economic and social progress occurred with the advent of the era of nations.

Supranational government is another temptation for the elites. In the salons of power the establishment speaks of the danger of democracy, the fact that people should not vote on issues they are unable to comprehend. The European Union has taken this attitude to the extreme, preventing the population from deciding on the construction of the institutions claimed to represent the people. From the standpoint of true human rights, this anti-democratic approach is not only contradictory, but indefensible. For a long time, when the policies implemented by the ruling class no longer had the consent of the people, that ruling class deserved to "lose the mandate of heaven," the term used by the Chinese to describe the revolts against a ruler who failed to guarantee the well-being of the people.

The restoration of national sovereignty, reviving the principle of Westphalia, could be the most effective response to the problems created by globalization. Rather than demonizing the existence of nations, it is necessary to recognize – as I have argued above – that the best way to face processes that otherwise seem ungovernable, and thus offer possibilities for private interests to manipulate the system to their own benefit, is through representative governments that function principally through national institutions. To paraphrase the famous quote attributed to Winston Churchill, the nation-state is the worst form of government, except for all those other forms that have been tried from time to time.

APPENDIX
BEYOND IDENTITY POLITICS[1]

The financial crisis of 2007-2008 represents a watershed moment for the United States, the moment when the concept of "identity politics" began to change. From that point on, it has become more difficult to define voters based on their ethnic group, gender, or other demographic characteristics, despite the widespread temptation to continue to do so. The popular response to major issues such as globalization, war, and corruption, increasingly cuts across the lines used by political analysts to segment the population, relegating wedge issues to the back burner.

This may seem counterintuitive in the Trump era: the president rails about the danger of immigration and criminals coming from abroad, and commentators often speak of the importance for Republicans of "angry white males." Yet, if we look below the surface, we see that the issues citizens care about the most are principally linked to the economy, although at times indirectly: the high cost of living, unstable work conditions, and the lack of certainty – and identity – in a changing world. As voters across the Western world deal with the effects of globalization, what unites us can become more important than what divides us, despite the bitter political split evident in daily politics. There is a need to rethink the current alignment in order to avoid repeating the same errors of the past three years. These are errors that have led the governing class to underestimate discontent in society, opening an abyss between the institutions and large swaths of the population, with considerable risks for social cohesion.

It's the economy, stupid! For the Republicans, too

The importance of campaigning on economic issues is certainly not new. James Carville's famous quip "It's the economy, stupid," explained

---

1   Originally appeared in Aspenia 83 "Il secondo tempo di Trump," published by Aspen Institute Italia, December 2018

the focus of Bill Clinton's political rhetoric. The difference today is that the right/left divide in the United States – in the past a synonym of the opposition between supporters of the free market and economic progressives, is changing. While the importance of the "socialist" wing of the Democratic Party is growing, on the other side of the political spectrum, things have been thrown into disarray. In 2016 the leadership of the GOP, for years the party seen as pro-business and against state intervention, was soundly beaten by a candidate who assailed the free market, invoking protectionism and also promising not to cut public programs such as Medicare and Medicaid, despite adopting the customary Republican criticisms of Obamacare.

It is interesting to note that even where Republicans are more "statist" – in military affairs – Donald Trump took a position that is anti-establishment, promising the end of useless wars in the Middle East in order to invest the money "wasted" abroad in the American economy. By beating 16 other candidates in the primaries, Trump demonstrated that the party's average voter is not actually linked to the political recipes espoused by their representatives. There is an ideological affinity, but when that affinity clashes with the realities of daily life, worries about the latter easily prevail. This does not mean the current president is a "leftist," but by presenting himself as an ideological conservative while emphasizing issues close to people's daily lives, he has succeeded in sowing mayhem for an establishment that, for years, enacted economic policies that evidently did not reflect the interests of its own base.

Not too far in the past – for example during the 2000 and 2004 election campaigns – a significant portion of the Republican electorate was mobilized based on the wedge issues of abortion and gay marriage. The attention to the latter, through the promotion of referendums in 11 states coinciding with the presidential election, may have been decisive in George W. Bush's re-election, considering his slim margin of victory in 2004 in the crucial state of Ohio, one where people went to vote on gay marriage.

Abortion and LGBT rights are still important for many voters, but opinion polls say that economic questions are at the top of the list, starting with the cost of health care. "Cultural" issues don't even crack the top ten. Today, you win if you can convince citizens that you will fight for them against the forces of an unequal and unjust society, a political system in which Wall Street and large corporations wield great power, creating the impression that the governing class ignores the needs of people who are less fortunate. Donald Trump succeeded in doing this in 2016, as did Barack Obama in 2008; in the second case, the explosion of the great financial crisis allowed an African-American candidate to exploit the rage and alarm for the economic situation, leading to a result that, if we were to think strictly in terms of identity, was unlikely.

Volumes have been written on the reaction of white Americans to Obama's victory, both immediately after the election, and in 2016. The essential argument, that angry white males sought to take power back from a minority president, is a gross exaggeration, an attempt to bring the political clash back onto more familiar ground. The current alignment is actually much simpler: winning candidates promise change with respect to a system that is not working for the majority of the population, allowing to overcome prejudice, that certainly exists, but is not decisive. The statistics say that 7-9 million Americans who voted for Obama then voted for Trump eight years later. Some researchers have suggested that those who followed this path have higher levels of racial hostility and xenophobia, deducing that race played a more incisive role than other factors.[2]

This argument is contradictory. Trump is said to confer legitimacy to racist sentiment, due to his rhetoric on immigrants, for example; but in looking back at 2008, the claim would have to be that many voters momentarily "forgot" they were racist when they voted for Obama.[3] Even if this were true, it would actually strengthen the proof that identity politics is relative. If concerns over the financial crisis prevailed over racial considerations – even only temporarily – then it is clear that these considerations are not always primary; they can change, if a candidate effectively appeals to other interests.

A negative demonstration of the same principle comes from the 2018 midterm elections. In the final weeks of the campaign in particular, President Trump concentrated on immigration, brandishing the danger of the famous migrant caravan that had departed from Honduras. The strategy essentially failed. Trump clearly aimed to mobilize his base to close the enthusiasm gap between Republicans and Democrats. This goal had already been partially achieved during the battle over the

---

2   See Tyler Reny, Loren Collingwood, Ali Valenzuela, 'Vote switching in the 2016 election: racial and immigration attitudes, not economics, explains shifts in white voting', in *Public Opinion Quarterly*.

3   Or, that they lied about having voted for him. The researchers find this possibility to be very small.

nomination of Brett Kavanaugh to the Supreme Court, and the president hoped to continue his success with one of his, apparently, most effective issues. The data from after the vote, however, shows that it didn't work; many undecideds were turned off by Trump's harsh rhetoric.[4]

This result could be attributed to a change in the electorate, with many no longer believing in a president who has not met their expectations in his first two years in office. Yet the same contradiction arises here: indicating race, and thus identity in a strict sense, as the dominant factor in political campaigns, means claiming that millions of citizens experienced an anti-racist moment in 2008, went back to being racist in 2016, and then changed direction again in 2018. Everything's possible, of course, and there is no denying the existence of racial prejudice in the United States, but the argument stands: this prejudice is not necessarily dominant, and takes a back seat when candidates are able to effectively appeal to voters' discontent in other areas.

What strategy for the Democrats?

In 2016, one of the largest mistakes made by Democratic strategists, and media analysts, was to assume that certain groups, such as Latinos, African-Americans and women, would support Hillary Clinton by overwhelming margins. This was not the case, or more precisely, the votes she received were insufficient to lead to victory. Clinton's strategy of counting on the rejection of Trump by various sub-groups of the population failed, even when those voters were part of categories often insulted by the Republican candidate. The idea of cobbling together a coalition of various social groups to defeat a candidate who spoke mainly to white, middle-aged and older men, did not work.

The same problem is evident today, after the 2018 midterms. The Democrats won; there was indeed a "blue wave," although not of historic proportions. In fact, the shift in the popular vote for the House of Representatives was approximately 8 percentage points, just 1 point above the average for midterm elections over the past seventy years. The challenge for the Democrats in defining their approach going forward

---

4   'Trump and Republicans: Xenophobia Backfired in the Midterms, So Let's Shut Down the Government Over an Unpopular Border Wall!' *America's Voice*, December 21, 2018.

is how to analyze the vote. If identity is the dominant factor, then it will be sufficient to continue with a strategy of a coalition of "tribes," that will inevitably become invincible with the growth of diversity of the population. If, on the other hand, these different identities do not guarantee a strong Democratic majority, but can be superseded by other issues, then the strategy must change.

The second scenario seems more likely. While the diversity of Democratic candidates has increased significantly – with more women, ethnic and social minorities – those candidates have mostly concentrated not on wedge issues, but on pocketbook issues: access to health care, the high cost of prescription drugs, and an increase in the minimum wage. If African-American candidates like Lucy McBath in Georgia and Colin Allred in Texas can win in suburbs where less than 15% of the population is black, it's clear that the content makes the candidate; the key is to recognize what works when asking people for their vote, not divide districts into good and bad, cosmopolitan and reactionary.

Identity in a globalized world

Identity is an important question, but it's important to more carefully define the meaning of the term. Recognizing trends in certain sectors of the population is useful and instructive, but human beings are not machines. The identity of a person does not end with the color of their skin, or even their sexual orientation. One well-known example of this contradiction is that of Latinos in the United States, many of whom are relatively recent immigrants. This so-called ethnic group often does not vote the way Democrats want, for various reasons, from religious background to the pride of having earned their position in the United States playing by the rules. In essence, the identity of an immigrant already in the United States for years, is not necessarily the same as a migrant who has just arrived.

To broaden the discussion to economic themes, we need to consider the identity of citizens in a globalized world. The post-industrial transformation of American society, the reduction of productive activities, and the uncertainty of employment in today's economy, has changed the sense of belonging of many Americans. In the past, a worker in the Midwest felt like part of a productive community, in a country with an important role in the world.

Globalization, and the financialization of the economy, have struck a blow to this sense of pride and belonging. A clear example comes from the issues used most effectively in the election campaigns of 2012 and 2016. Mitt Romney was damaged considerably by the focus on his role as a manager of Bain Capital, when he was responsible for various company restructuring operations. The "Coffin" television advertisement, in which a worker told of how Romney and his company earned more than 100 million dollars by closing a factory in Ohio, was devastating. In 2016, Trump's use of the case of Carrier in Indiana, that despite taking large public subsidies had announced plans to move part of its production to Mexico, helped define his battle in favor of American manufacturing.

To some, "Make America Great Again" may seem like a superficial slogan, but for millions of people it evokes an idea of the United States contrary to the difficulties in today's global society, with new types of pressures and changes that undermine adequate protections for much of the population. Although the slogan is associated personally with Donald Trump, it would be a mistake to blame the messenger, and ignore the fundamental issue: in a world where economic well-being and certainty has been eroded by a system that enhances inequality, the identity of a people, that recalls the positive characteristics of a country, is a factor able to upend political categories, and become more important than identity considered more narrowly.

MIMESIS GROUP
www.mimesis-group.com

MIMESIS INTERNATIONAL
www.mimesisinternational.com
info@mimesisinternational.com

MIMESIS EDIZIONI
www.mimesisedizioni.it
mimesis@mimesisedizioni.it

ÉDITIONS MIMÉSIS
www.editionsmimesis.fr
info@editionsmimesis.fr

MIMESIS COMMUNICATION
www.mim-c.net

MIMESIS EU
www.mim-eu.com

Printed by Digital Team - Fano (PU)
April 2019